EMPTY HANDS

EMPTY HANDS

A Memoir

ONE WOMAN'S JOURNEY TO SAVE CHILDREN ORPHANED BY AIDS IN SOUTH AFRICA

Sister Abegail Ntleko

Foreword by Desmond Tutu

Afterword by Kittisaro *and* Thanissara

North Atlantic Books
Berkeley, California

Published by
North Atlantic Books
Berkeley, California

Cover design by Jasmine Hromjak
Book design by Mary Ann Casler and Jasmine Hromjak
Printed in the United States of America

Cover photo © 2012 by Stefano Massei
Photos courtesy of Sister Abegail Ntleko
Photo with the Dalai Lama by Michael Yamashita

Original story written with the help of Storyzon, a California-based company whose mission is to commemorate and celebrate life stories and personal histories.

Some names and identifying details have been changed to protect the privacy of individuals.

Empty Hands, A Memoir: One Woman's Journey to Save Children Orphaned by AIDS in South Africa is sponsored and published by the Society for the Study of Native Arts and Sciences (dba North Atlantic Books), an educational nonprofit based in Berkeley, California, that collaborates with partners to develop cross-cultural perspectives, nurture holistic views of art, science, the humanities, and healing, and seed personal and global transformation by publishing work on the relationship of body, spirit, and nature.

North Atlantic Books' publications are available through most bookstores. For further information, visit our website at www.northatlanticbooks.com or call 800-733-3000.

Library of Congress Cataloging-in-Publication Data

Ntleko, Abegail, Sister, author.
    Empty hands, a memoir : one woman's journey to save children orphaned by AIDS in South Africa / Sister Abegail Ntleko ; foreword by Desmond Tutu ; afterword by Kittisaro and Thanissara.
        p. ; cm.
    Summary: "Now 79 years old, Sister Abegail looks back over her life and recounts the remarkable events that led to her becoming the mother of dozens of children orphaned by the AIDS crisis in South Africa"—Provided by publisher.
    ISBN 978-1-58394-932-0 (paperback) — ISBN 978-1-58394-933-7 (E-book)
    I. Society for the Study of Native Arts and Sciences, sponsoring body. II. Title.
    [DNLM: 1. Ntleko, Abegail, Sister. 2. Acquired Immunodeficiency Syndrome—history—South Africa. 3. HIV Infections—history—South Africa. 4. Nurses—South Africa—Autobiography. 5. Adoption—South Africa. 6. Child, Orphaned—South Africa. 7. History, 20th Century—South Africa. 8. History, 21st Century—South Africa. WZ 100]

    362.19697'920092—dc23
    [B]

2015001728

1 2 3 4 5 6 7 UNITED 19 18 17 16 15

Printed on recycled paper

In gratitude to my parents and the entire Ntleko clan,
and with love to all my children

Contents

Foreword by Desmond Tutu   xi

1. Legs to Stand   1

2. Wings to Fly   19

3. Hands to Hold   37

4. The AIDS Crisis   67

5. Hope and Rising Up   83

6. Rewards   103

7. Transitions   111

8. Empty Hands   119

Afterword by Kittisaro and Thanissara   123

Acknowledgments   127

Illustrations

1. The rondavel where Abegail grew up.
2. Mancini, Abegail's mother.
3. Paternal aunt Adelaide.
4. Paternal aunt Matha, who died at 104.
5. Abegail's graduation from the University of Natal, 1989.
6. Family of Reverend Johanson, who helped Abegail find holiday jobs to fund her purchase of clothing and other necessities.
7. Abegail at age twenty, working as a domestic servant in Port Shepstone.
8. Sister Abegail (center) with Sisters Jane Ngcobo and Khle Dlamini, 1966.
9. Sister Abegail (far right) at Elim Hospital in northern Polokwane.
10. Abegail's graduation from the University of Natal.
11. Abegail, age thirty-six, at nursing school graduation.
12. Abe at thirty-two (right) with friend Doris Bekwa.
13. Abegail with first group of adopted orphans.
14. Happy moments with children at Clouds.
15. One big family.
16. On the jungle gym donated by community members.
17. Busisiwe, 2009.
18. Busisiwe and brother, 2009.

19. Training community care workers.
21. Abegail on the way to a lecture about AIDS, 2005.
22. Abegail with a plaque in her honor at the youth center in Mqatsheni.
23. Abegail receives an Exploration Award, which was given to nurses for outstanding community service and outreach, 1979.
24. At Clouds, 2009.
25.   In London, dancing the "Shosholoza," 2009.
26. Sister Abegail receives the Unsung Heroes of Compassion Award from the Dalai Lama in 2009.

Foreword

It is with great joy that I introduce the reader to Sister Abegail Ntleko and *Empty Hands,* a wonderful story of Abegail's life and work. Sister Abegail and I share faith in the fundamental goodness of God's deeper mystery. It is from this profound source of in-spiration that her life and work have flowed. Throughout the book we learn of the courage, wit, wisdom, and strength that Sister Abegail has brought to bear on challenges that would have undone the best of us. We also rejoice in her many victories on behalf of the vulnerable through a dedicated life of community service.

The capacity of the heart never fails to amaze me. Sister Abegail exemplifies the true heart of South Africa—a heart that overcame Apartheid, that sees the best within all people, and that has never closed in the face of suffering. Her openness and her hard-earned nursing skills allowed Sister Abegail to quickly grasp the implications of the AIDS pandemic at a very early stage of its arrival into our consciousness. Since then, she has not faltered in finding ways of responding through ministering to the sick, educating her community, and establishing homes for the orphaned and vulnerable. Sister Abegail's fight against AIDS has saved the lives of many and inspired even more. Her work is the vivid response of the compassionate heart.

We sometimes accomplish great things regardless of where and how we grew up, regardless of what we were told was possible. Hope can rise from the most adverse circumstances. The life and work of Sister Abegail Ntleko show that. Her story tells us what a single person can accomplish when heart and mind work together in the service of others. Hers is a remarkable tale of what it means to be fully human. It is people like Sister Abegail who usher in a better future for South Africa.

—REVEREND ARCHBISHOP DESMOND TUTU
JULY 2012

Twenty-four brand-new hours are before me.
I vow to live fully in each moment
and to look at all beings with eyes of compassion.

—THICH NHAT HANH

1

Legs to Stand

I always loved the smell of fresh cow dung. Some families preferred mud, but we always used dung. To keep the floor of our hut tidy, we would rub in a new layer of manure every week. I'd sit on my knees and spread the dung in wide circling movements and then press and rub it in until the floor became all smooth and shiny. There wouldn't be a speck of dust on it! To this day, I love that rich, earthy smell.

Our rondavel, or hut, consisted of just one round room made from mud blocks with a thatched roof. It needed constant maintenance. When a mud block would split, we had to smear in fresh mud to patch it up. When the roof started leaking, we would gather green twigs and then have somebody bend them into form and weave them onto the thatch where the hole was. All the families had to do that.

We didn't need much furniture. All we had were a couple of tree stumps for chairs, which my dad would cut according to the children's varying heights, and a pillar post with cracks, where we would stick our spoons and knives. That was very practical because the knives could be stuck in high enough so that the smallest children couldn't reach them. In the center of the hut was the fireplace with a large cooking pot over it. Rondavels typically didn't have windows, and since the fire was going much of the time, it was always pretty smoky.

We lived outside a place called Harding in KwaZulu-Natal, South Africa, just about fifty miles from the coast. Today, Harding is a small town with a number of shops and even a golf course, but back then it was pretty rural. My mother gave birth to thirteen children. I was the twelfth. The baby who came after me died as an infant, so I was the youngest in the family.

My mother's name always makes me smile: Mancini, which means "small girl." When I think of Mancini, my heart opens wide.

Shortly after giving birth to her last child, my mother died. Of course, all of us children had been born at home. I don't know if there even was a hospital, but if there was, people were too scared to go. The bleeding from that last delivery never really stopped, I was told, and my mother eventually died from anemia. I was three and a half years old.

I don't recall her face, but I am very lucky to have a photo I can remember her by. It shows a tremendously kind face with large dark eyes. It is also fortunate that she had a twin brother who looked just like her, so I could always see a bit of her in him. She was from the same area I grew up in and was one of nine children.

My relatives spoke of her with great fondness. Though she wasn't educated, it seems she was a kind person, quiet and loving, ready to help wherever and whenever she could. She not only took care of her own children but also looked after other people's, just to help out. And she worked very hard to support our family. Besides running the household, she baked and sewed and did other handwork for ladies who were getting married, and she also did the washing and ironing for a nearby farm. It couldn't have been easy for poor Mancini. She had married young, probably at age sixteen or seventeen, and by the time she passed in her early forties, seven of her children had already died. But the people she left behind remembered a woman who was dearly loved.

My father wasn't an easy man to live with. He drank like a fish and smoked like a chimney. He spent virtually all of his money on alcohol and dagga, cannabis. When I was old enough to climb onto a horse, I often had to ride out in the middle of the night to fetch him from wherever his drinking spree had taken him. I would find somebody to lift him onto the horse, and then I'd walk the horse home. He wasn't a bad person, and he was a very loving father, but he'd just had some bad luck in life and no skills to deal with it.

My mother had been his third wife; the first two had also died. Since he never had much of an education and jobs were hard to come by in the Harding area, he had to go to work in the diamond mines outside of Johannesburg. He really tried to provide for us, but after just a few years, the dust of the mines got into his lungs and he developed pneumoconiosis. I think he already had asthma, and when he contracted the lung disease, it left him physically crippled and unfit for work. The mining company promised him a disability grant of five shillings every three months and sent him home. So there he was, just sitting at home, unable to work or keep himself busy. It wasn't good for him and soon he started to develop bad habits. When I was maybe ten or twelve, I asked him, "Why are you drinking? What do you get from being drunk?" and he said, "It's how I am consoling myself for all the hard times I've had." To lose three wives so early in life, to see thirteen of your children die (all six children from his first wife), and to have your health ruined while trying to feed the remaining children was more than he could take.

After my mother died, distant relatives took the youngest of my brothers, and my oldest sister took care of the rest of us. But pretty soon my sister got married and left the house too. Then the next sister left to work someplace. One after another, all my siblings moved away, and by the time I was six I was left alone with my dad. He decided that it was best for us to live closer to his sister, so he built a small hut not too far from her place. I think he wanted her to help raise and feed me, but my aunt had children of her own and she too was very poor. Often there wasn't enough food for everybody, and my aunt couldn't help us out. With my dad out drinking all the time, I was pretty much left to fend for myself. It was time for me to grow up, and to do it fast.

My father may not have been much of a provider or a role model. He was an uneducated man, and later in life—when I was a teenager—it would take all my strength to rebel against him. But underneath his short-comings, he was a dad who could be funny and insight-ful, even wise, and what's more, he adored his children. I think what we choose to remember in a man ulti-mately becomes that person. And while from a distance my dad may not have been the greatest father, in my heart I know that he loved us as best as he knew how.

When he wasn't brooding over his misfortunes or out drinking, he liked to tell stories and jokes. He had an endless repertoire of magical tales full of giants and fairies, and he would tell these stories with great ani-mation and warmth. I also learned a number of little tricks from him that I would later in life use with my own children. For example, when he wanted me to fall asleep, he would tell a story in which somebody had to climb up a hill—up and up and up—repeating the line over and over. Of course, that would put me to sleep, and if I happened to wake up, I would anxiously ask, "Dad, are they still going up?" And he would calmly say, "Yes, dear, they are still going up and up and up."

Sometimes my father tried to teach me something of life, to share some understanding with me. He wouldn't sit me down and simply lecture me but rather would find a way to make it vivid and appropriate for my age.

One day—I can't remember how old I was—he called me over to him. "Bring me some sand," he said, "just shovel it up with your hands." Arms stretched out, hands filled with sand, I walked up to him. He looked at me, smiling, and calmly started peeling a banana. "Would you like this?" he asked, offering the banana to me. I nodded but was a bit confused. "What should I do with the sand in my hands?" "Well," he said, "when your hands are already full, it's hard to receive something, isn't it? You need to let go first. Remember, you can receive in life only when your hands are empty." This was the way he would teach me.

For the most part, however, I was alone. Nights were often difficult because I was scared of the dark. My savior and best friend was Chomi, our dog. I don't know how I would have made it without him. My life-long love for animals started with Chomi. When my father left at night, I requested that he at least leave me Chomi, and he did. Chomi not only protected me but was also somebody to talk to. When there was no food in the house, I would discuss matters with Chomi. "Chomi, what are we going to eat? There is nothing in the house. What do you think we should do?" One time, I was so hungry that I went over to my aunt's, but she only shook her head and said, "Your dad is drinking away all the money. Why should I take care of his children?" One thing I could do was boil grains—my hands were still too small for the heavy grinding stones used to make grain into flour for baking. If I had a little milk from herding cattle during the day, I would pour that over the grain. Then Chomi and I would sit together by the fire and share the food.

I quickly learned that if I wanted to eat, I had to earn the food myself. Initially I herded cattle, milked cows, picked grains, helped with the harvest, or simply searched through already harvested fields for lost beans or forgotten potatoes. What else could a girl of six or seven do?

It wasn't easy to make the time for earning a living because I also had to do all of the household chores and serve my father. I had to gather firewood and fetch water, cook meals, do laundry, and keep the house not only clean but also intact. The water, for example, had to be fetched in a bucket from a well that was about a kilometer away. To make things worse, it was also down a pretty steep hill from where we lived. A bucket full of water can become very heavy for a young girl! Whenever I made it back up the hill, I would always be sweating and panting. And worst of all, half of the water had usually spilled from all the movement. Then I would stoke a fire and prepare a meal. Of course, I didn't know much about cooking, so I just tried to teach myself, and sometimes a neighbor would show me what to do.

Once a week, I would do laundry down at the river, which was about two kilometers away. I would wash the clothes and hang them up for drying so they wouldn't be so heavy to carry back. During the time it took for them to dry I would take my weekly bath. I'd go downstream maybe another kilometer—it was bad luck, we were told, to wash yourself in the same spot where you did your laundry. There was a special kind of stone I rubbed my skin with. It was supposed to make the skin smoother so you could wipe the water off more easily—after all, we didn't have towels. It makes me giggle when I think that today, more than sixty years later, people pay a lot of money to have a "scrub" in a spa. I guess I had my own spa treatment every week!

Once a week, the floor in our hut had to be redone. There was just always something to do, so it was hard to find enough time to work for our food.

When I was older, maybe ten or eleven, I was able to start doing more demanding tasks such as working the fields. By then we owned a couple of milk cows, two oxen, and a small piece of land. Two oxen weren't enough to till the land though, so I would borrow two more from our neighbor, plow the land, then sow— maize, pumpkin, or sorghum—and later in the year reap it. Usually the neighbors would help me, and I in turn would help the neighbors.

From the time we had our own cows, we had more than enough milk. This was wonderful, because it meant not only that I was no longer hungry but also that we had enough to share with other children and women who had trouble breastfeeding. My father was very generous and always encouraged me to offer milk to anybody who needed it. This was fun for me, because it meant that I could invite other children to come over. Sometimes they would come when I had made some maize, and then we would sit in a circle, pour milk over the maize, and eat together. I loved hosting these little parties.

There still was no time for me to really play though. I could see other children playing games, but of course they didn't have as many chores as I did. Occasionally I was asked to sing or dance at a wedding. An older girl from the village would come to our home and ask my father for permission to practice with me for a few hours in the afternoon, and then I would perform for the wedding couple. I liked that.

Music has always been a great joy for me. Of course, there was no money to buy an instrument, but it wasn't too difficult to build my own. I took an old five-gallon tin container and drilled a hole into it the size of an orange. Then I cut a bunch of long hair from my dad's horse's tail and twirled it into strings. All I had to do then was take a plank the width of my hand, attach it to the container, string the horsehair, and I was ready to go. Though I never learned how to read music, I taught myself how to play a little and sang along.

For the most part, I didn't really have friends. It wasn't that I didn't get along with other children, there was just no time to make friends. I don't think I ever felt lonely or begrudged my fate though. My life was just different, and there wasn't much time to feel sorry for myself. I had one beautiful friend, Chomi. And if I ever needed to cheer myself up, I would take the guitar out and play. So there I'd be, sitting with Chomi next to me by the evening fire, playing my guitar. Usually I was so tired from the day that I didn't last very long, and it was so nice to be able to stretch out and sleep. That was my reward. I probably didn't have much of what people think of as a childhood, but I can't say that I ever felt any regrets.

Life wasn't easy. And yet, as far back as I can remember, there were always wonderful people who helped out along the way. I am grateful for all the kindness and generosity I experienced, for the spirit of *ubuntu.*

When I was a child in the 1930s, the social fabric of Zulu culture was more or less intact, meaning the community would watch out for individuals and try to prevent the worst from happening. If, for example, a child lost both parents, the chief of the community would look around for parents who had lost a child and then ask them to take care of the orphan. Or if a child lost just one parent, people from the village would frequently come and check on the child. I remember people coming up to our hut and asking me, "Do you have any problems? Please let us know if we can help." Of course, I usually told them that I was all right because I didn't want anybody to know if I wasn't. But the truth was that they often did help, and I couldn't have managed some things without them.

The area around Harding is rather flat and covered mainly with grass. In June, July, and August, fierce winds come down and sweep the landscape with particular might. Everything that isn't attached will blow away, and nothing, no mountains or forests, tamp down this force of nature. I remember sitting in the night, frightened, listening to the ferocious howling outside, praying that our hut would withstand the violence. When a roof was damaged, it was important to take care of it immediately, because if you didn't, the next storm around the corner would mercilessly rip through any opening. But how could a small child fix a roof that was ripped apart by the wind? She couldn't. So after every storm, people from the village came, assessed the damage, and helped with repairs. Ubuntu.

Ubuntu is really quite a beautiful way of looking at things. It is the Zulu understanding that you are a person because of other people, and it is the reason for your helping others and others helping you. It's really a very old idea that started long before industrialization. We have a saying in Zulu that one hand helps the other. If you want to wash one hand, the other hand needs to help. Ubuntu is not a moral obligation; rather, it's a natural sense that we are all in this together, a sense of belonging to a community, that by doing for others, you help yourself.

For me, support and kindness also came from people outside of our community. One such person was a young Englishwoman named Margaret McKechnie, who ran a nearby mission. I would call her "Mom" because she was indeed like a mother to me. Thinking of her makes my heart open wide. She would often come and check on me, talk to me, hold me. She would also organize black women from our area to come and help. I remember one day the plank door to our rondavel had fallen apart, and instead of replacing it, my father simply hung a sack where the door used to be. I didn't like that because I was scared without a door at night. One day, Ms. McKechnie came and saw that the door was missing. "Why didn't you tell me?" she said. And the next day, men from the mission came and put in a new door. She was the one who gave me my first pair of shoes when I was eighteen. And it was she who taught me something that would guide me for the rest of my life: if you want to be of help and service to others, you need to first get an education; otherwise, you are the one who will need the help. Ms. McKechnie watched over me for many, many years. She died in London at age 103.

Community meant more than just help; it also organized events and gatherings to provide entertainment and education and to keep the boys from idling around and having bad thoughts. Every Friday, there was a dance. Oh, Zulu dances are ferocious! People play drums and horns, and the men and women perform their wild dances, jumping, stomping on the ground, and shouting out loud. Before the dances, we would get together with our mentors, an older-girl mentor for the girls and an older-boy mentor for the boys. They'd sit us down and tell us how to take care of ourselves; for girls it was about how to protect our virginity and so on. Similarly, the boys were taught the principles of soma, the honor that young men derive from not sleeping with their chosen girl before marriage.

There were other mechanisms in place to ensure that the traditional values of Zulu society were kept up. For example, we girls had to undergo regular virginity tests, the last one of which takes place on the morning of your wedding. As teenagers we were far from being bothered by these tests; on the contrary, we were proud to prove that we had been good girls. Later, I would find the system rather archaic, as I had to undergo the checks as a young adult. Yet I can also see that more mechanisms like these may have helped prevent or at least control the HIV/AIDS crisis that was to ravage our communities.

Though much of what I learned growing up has helped me in my adult life, not everything about traditional Zulu culture was positive. For example, girls are usually not allowed to go to school. Folklore has it that when a girl gets an education, she will run away, embark on a ship, and never come back. I don't know where that story comes from, but its point is quite simple: girls are the property of their parents—their fathers in particular; they have no right to run off and do what they see fit. Girls have to work for the family until they are old enough to be married off. Then they start working for their husband and his family. My father was very traditional in this belief. He was not Zulu but Xhosa and had moved to Harding from Eastern Cape. I sometimes wonder whether he felt that he had to be particularly strict with the local customs to demonstrate how well he fit in.

This attitude toward girls was a problem for me, as I always wanted to be educated. I wanted to go to school.

As long as I can think back, I had a burning desire to learn. It seemed to me that an education would be my only way out, my one chance to create a life of my own making. Ms. McKechnie had shown me that life could be different, but in order to walk that other path, I needed to be educated.

My determination only grew when I saw what happened to one of my sisters after her marriage. Her husband often beat her for no apparent reason, and she became little more than a slave to him. One day, she came to our hut, bleeding badly. We knew she was pregnant, so we were very worried. "Why don't you go to a hospital?" my father said. "My husband told me I mustn't," she replied. She was so submissive. Then we found out that this man had stood on her abdomen and that the placenta had started secreting. Soon after, she gave birth to an abnormal child who died a few days later. This man was torturing her cruelly, and she would just take it and even cover up for him. I was determined to never be treated like that; I would never be a man's slave. An education would give me independence. I thought, If I am educated, I can still get married. If things don't work out with a man, at least I have other options.

Back then, men could do with their wives pretty much as they pleased, and the inequality started very early on. In Zulu culture, girls would go naked until they started menstruating. When a girl went to the river to wash herself, it was common for the boys to follow her and watch her. They would call out, "Turn this way, turn that way!" and the girl had to obey. It was as if they were checking produce at the market. When a boy eventually decided to marry, he paid the bride's father labola, a dowry, and with that he pretty much owned the girl. I just knew that I had to do everything in my power to prevent that from being my fate, and going to school was the necessary first step.

I begged my father again and again to let me go to school, but he wouldn't have it. Ms. McKechnie talked to him on my behalf but to no avail. In the meantime, I was constantly reminded of why I needed to learn how to read and write. In Sunday school, most of the children already knew how to read, and when the teacher told us to learn a verse for the following week, say John 3:16 from the New Testament, I would desperately try to count with my fingers and toes to figure out what that meant. Then I would have to go to the other children and ask them to please read the verse to me, and they would sometimes laugh and say, "Not now, I don't have time." I wanted to learn what the teacher had asked us to learn, but how could I?

On another occasion, I got a letter from a friend in Johannesburg. I took the letter to the man who read for all the uneducated people whenever they received something in writing. He looked at the letter and started laughing and teasing me in public, saying, "Oh, this must be your boyfriend, let's see what he has to say." I felt humiliated; this man had no business making fun of me. I just knew I had to learn how to read and write myself.

My determination was fueled by another desire that was nearly as strong as my desire for independence: I wanted to be able to help people. As a woman in traditional Zulu culture, your family is your chief concern. You take care of your children and your husband. Now, that's a good thing; it's wonderful to take care of your family. But I wanted to help more people, I wanted to help the whole community; I wanted to help everybody who was in need of help. Again, I knew getting an education would help me be able to do that. If only my father would let me go to school!

But he simply didn't believe girls needed to be or should be educated, and he wasn't in the minority. In the 1940s, only about a third of all children in our area went to school and very few of them were girls. Plus, my father was probably afraid he would lose his caregiver. Who would take care of the house, the cows, and the field? Who would cook and clean and wash? It was a girl's duty to stay with her family and work to the best of her abilities. No discussion.

So every time I asked him, he flat-out refused. I saw other children leave for school in the morning and looked after them longingly. Then I would go again to my father, just to be rejected. Year after year I stubbornly renewed my request and equally stubbornly he would tell me, "No, this isn't going to happen." But instead of discouraging me, each rejection made my determination grow stronger. Eventually I was willing to risk what then seemed almost unthinkable: open rebellion against my father.

When I was fourteen years old, I finally understood that nothing would ever change unless I took matters into my own hands. I had to act. Come what may, I would not waver. Going to school secretly was impossible, and my father wasn't going to change his mind. Either he needed to be forced or I would have to run away. Either way, it meant my being openly defiant.

So I decided to go and talk to the *induna*, the chief of our community. You could call him the mayor of our town. I humbly requested to speak with him, and the man kindly listened to my request and promised to see what he could do for me. Then he called a meeting with my father and asked that I be present. I was very nervous and barely dared to speak. My father was angry that I had involved the chief, and I think he felt betrayed by me. The chief asked me to repeat my request. It took all the courage I had, but I looked my father in the eye and asked. Then the chief spoke. He told me that it was my first duty to fulfill my obligations at home—all of them. I would need to keep sowing and harvesting, cleaning and cooking, and running the household. But, he said, if I could keep up with all my obligations, then he would ask my father to let me attend school. In addition to that, he would see to it that my virginity would be checked regularly, at least every month and after each social gathering, to make sure I didn't go astray. Begrudgingly, my father consented that if these conditions were met, he would let me go to school. Honestly, I don't think he felt I could possibly manage to find the time to both go to school and keep up my duties.

For the next few weeks, I thought about what I needed to do. I would need to cut down on my sleep and do some of the chores before school. No problem. I would need to talk to the neighbor kids and see if they would watch our cattle while I was in school; in return, I would promise to watch theirs over the weekend. Laundry, cleaning, and other chores could be done on the weekends too. No problem. If I didn't go to any more dances, that would give me a few additional hours here and there. If I went to bed later, I could study at night. No problem. Virginity tests? Also, not a problem. I certainly had no intention of fooling around. I prepared, organized, coordinated. I worked very, very hard. Finally, the day came when my father couldn't refuse any longer to let me go. I was exhausted but at the same time bursting with excitement. I was fourteen years old when I entered first grade. When I left in the morning, my father didn't wave good-bye. It didn't matter. This was my day.

Looking back, I think I understood something that day. I understood something that would influence and shape my entire life: If I persisted in my aspirations— regardless of how difficult they were or how unlikely their success seemed—if only I persisted and kept my focus on what I wanted to do and what was right, eventually I could do anything.

2

Wings to Fly

At fourteen, I was one of the older students in the class, but I was not the oldest. With us was an adult man who worked somewhere close to Devon and already had his own children. I asked him, "Mr. Morgan, why are you here with us?" He said, "My child, I'm tired of counting trucks by using sticks!" He explained that he was responsible for checking in trucks full of goods, and he would use different colored sticks to represent the number of goods in each load. Often, the drivers would accuse him of mixing up the numbers and nobody would believe him when his only proof was his sticks, so he wanted to learn how to count properly.

For school, girls were expected to wear a clean dress, and all students needed to bring a slate and a slate pencil. My father didn't have the money for any of this, so I found a farm nearby where I was allowed to work all day weeding maize. At the end of the day, I received one tickey, or threepence—enough to buy a little bit of fabric and a slate.

My first day at school didn't quite go as I thought it would. To start the day, a teacher took all the first-graders and asked them what they wanted to do when they finished school. "I want to be a nurse," I said when it was my turn. He looked at me, incredulous at first, and then burst out laughing. "Now, here is a child! How old are you?" "Fourteen." "And you want to become a nurse?" "Yes." Now, all the students joined in laughing, and the teacher wrote what I said on a piece of paper and handed it to me. "Go to this-and-that class," he said, "and give it to your teacher." So I did, and when that teacher saw the note, he too started laughing and mocking me. I remember the entire class was laughing and laughing as if they had never heard anything funnier. They figured I would be in my mid-twenties before I could even start high school and so a nursing degree would probably take until my mid-thirties. Considering that girls usually married around age sixteen, this idea seemed impossible to them. I was hurt, but I remembered something my father once told me: "When people laugh at you, it's because they only see the outside, they don't know what's inside you." Well, the class knew my age and understood the math of my situation correctly, but I guess they didn't know what was inside me.

Whitbey Memorial School was part of the missionary compound that also housed the local clinic. There were thirty-six children in my class, but we often had "visitors," meaning children from other classes joined us for a period of time. Our classroom was quite neat. We all sat in rows at wooden desks (the kind you can open from the front), with our slates and crayons ready to go. I usually went from eight in the morning until half past two. In the beginning, no food was offered, and because I didn't have enough food to bring with me, I was often quite hungry. But then the mission started handing out meals, usually fried maize and beans, which are very nutritious, so we were well fed. I was very focused and became an excellent student. It's not that I was so much smarter than the other students, I just had the one big advantage of knowing the value of learning something. When other children made noise or acted out, I would reprimand them—I wasn't there to fool around and have fun. When others played games, I didn't let myself get distracted. I wanted to learn. It had been so hard to get this opportunity. I wasn't going to let it go to waste.

From age fifteen on, young men occasionally showed interest in marrying me. I would always try to discourage them. "Why would you want to marry somebody from a rondavel that's falling apart? Think about all the labola you'd have to pay! And then there are presents for the in-laws, and you have to have blankets, buy basins—it would be so expensive." If that method didn't work, I would tell them straightforwardly, "Look, I am very sorry, but I am trying to educate myself, and I am not going to stop. I don't see myself getting married at this age." Funny enough, for once my father and I agreed. He never even tried to push me into marriage. Maybe he knew that once I was married, I wouldn't be able to help him with the household anymore. Maybe he was appalled by what his oldest daughter was suffering at the hands of her husband. Whatever the reason, he never tried to force me, and I had no intention of letting marriage get in the way of my education.

By this time, my relationship with my father had steered back into calmer waters. He still didn't think it was right that I was going to school, but he was happy that I had stayed with him. He genuinely enjoyed being with me, and I'm sure he was glad I continued to run the household for him. The nights he happened to stay at home were usually quite harmonious. After dinner, we'd sit around the fire and he would contentedly watch me study.

I attended school until I was eighteen and had just finished fourth grade, when something happened that would make me run away from home and change my life as I knew it: school uniforms were introduced.

Until that point, all a girl needed to attend school was a dress—preferably clean and without holes. Schools were traditionally run by missionaries (even if the government paid the salaries). But now, the state was taking greater control of the school system, and by the mid-1950s, the British uniform system was introduced. A girl was now required to have a tunic or gym dress, a khaki shirt, shoes, and so on. I had never owned a pair of shoes, so how was I to get one? But even if I did, the material for the gym clothing alone was two tickeys (sixpence) a yard. For one full day of work, I would get only one tickey, and it would have been very hard for me to make the time for that. To pay for the full uniform I would have needed weeks of work. My dad was always penniless, and besides, I don't think he would have paid for the clothes anyway.

So this was bad news. All I wanted was to be educated, and now—in spite of my good marks—I wasn't even going to be able to continue through high school. All that was left to do was go back to what I had been doing before school—herding cattle and serving my father. The only alternative seemed to be marriage, meaning herding cattle and serving somebody else, plus having children. The more I pondered my situation, the more desperate I became. What was I to do? I realized there was no solution to my dilemma if I stayed where I was. It was out of the question that my father would ever let me leave, so the only way out was to run away and try to find a job somewhere that would allow me to make enough money to buy what I needed to go back to school.

The decision to run away was fraught with emotional, moral, and even legal issues; since 1952, black people hadn't been allowed to move freely within South Africa. I knew my father would be terribly upset with me, and I wasn't sure whether I even had the right to be so selfish as to run away and follow my own wishes. On the other hand, I strongly believed I had to follow my dream, and there was just no other way to do that. So I devised a plan to run away.

I would have to leave the house very early in the morning. To make sure my father wouldn't get suspicious, I made it my new habit to get up before dawn every day. For a couple of weeks prior to actually taking off, I rose early and left to fetch water or gather firewood. The night before my departure, I carefully packed my few belongings and hid them outside in a ditch. In the morning, I acted as normally as possible, although my heart was beating very fast, and without saying a word I left. I hurried to pick up my bundle, met up with Veronica, a neighbor girl who also wanted to run away, and off we went. We had decided to go to Port Shepstone, a coastal town about sixty kilometers from Harding. During the summer months, there was a bit of tourism there, and we hoped we might find jobs. As a safeguard, I knew of a maternal aunt living in Port Shepstone, and Veronica had some relatives there as well.

Fortunately, I easily found a family in Port Shepstone, the Kings, who took me in to watch over their little girl, Andrea. I told the Kings, "I ran away from home. If the police come, please don't tell them anything." The family was very kind to me. It was the first white family I'd worked for, and they paid me well and took good care of me. When I started, I asked them to not give me any of my salary, not a pence, but rather to save it up for me. I figured this way I wouldn't even be tempted to spend any money. When we went to the market and Andrea asked her parents to buy me something, I would urge them, "Please don't, I'd rather save the money." They kept their promise and saved the money for me. They were good people. And there was another benefit to staying with this family. I learned something from them that would prove invaluable later in life: English.

As I mentioned earlier, my father came from Eastern Cape and spoke Xhosa, so that's the language I grew up with. In elementary school we all spoke Zulu. This wasn't hard for me to learn, because it's quite similar to Xhosa. But I knew that in high school and college, only English was allowed. In fact, the high school I would later attend even employed "linguistic spies," students who walked around to overhear what others said, and, if they caught a word of Zulu, reported the offender. The language requirement posed a problem for me, because English wasn't taught in grammar school and very few people I knew spoke it. I'd tried to pick it up from the occasional words I'd heard, but that hadn't amounted to much. Andrea's parents wanted me to speak only in English to the child, so they talked to me in English too. This was my opportunity! I tried to absorb as much as I could, and this way I learned the foundation. Of course, I didn't study it properly, so my English never became very polished. But I learned enough to speak with fluency and ease, enough to eventually move on in the educational system.

I worked in Port Shepstone for a little more than a year before I returned home. As I expected, my father was not happy with me. The first thing he did was send me to an old lady who worked for the head man to have my virginity tested. Only when she confirmed that yes, I was fine, did he calm down a bit. With some of the money that I had saved up, I bought blankets for him and myself, and I also got him a new shirt and a pair of trousers. I think that all helped to appease him.

My plan was to go back to school as soon as possible, so I knew that I would need to make some additional money in order for us to survive in the long term. I thought about how I could use my small savings to start a little business and decided to buy a couple of baby chickens. My father helped take care of them and after some time my neighbor sold them at the market. From the proceedings, I bought more baby chicks and so on. It worked out well, and the business afforded me enough income to provide for my father and myself for the next couple of years. And most importantly, I could return to school!

I was allowed to skip one grade, so I reentered primary school at the sixth-grade level. For two years, I continued to live with my father until I completed eighth grade, but after that there were some tough decisions to be made.

I was twenty-three years old and wanted to continue my education. Where we lived, however, there wasn't a high school nearby, meaning I would have to leave again. And if I wanted to get married, this was perhaps my last chance. If I went on to high school and then nursing school, I would be well into my thirties before I would finish my schooling—and no one would marry a woman who was that old. No wonder that some ten years earlier the teachers and students had laughed at me: to them, a woman who didn't marry was hardly considered a real woman.

I weighed my options, but to my surprise I found that this time the decision wasn't all that difficult. Ever since I was a young teen I'd had a dream. I wanted to be able to work with communities and to help people. I wanted to be of service but not be the servant of a husband. I was a half orphan and from a very poor family, but I'd already done more than anyone had expected. I was not going to give up now.

A few years earlier, at age seventeen, something had happened that would now prove to be of great help: I had become a Christian.

My British missionary mother, Ms. McKechnie, had asked my dad for permission to take me to summer camp, and to my big surprise he'd allowed me to go. It was then that I'd accepted Christ as my personal savior. This was a big step for me. It wasn't so much that I had some sudden spiritual awakening. I just deeply admired the Christians I knew. There seemed to be a purity in their desire to help, a sense of kindness and selflessness that spoke to me. And I liked that they ran schools and tried to get children educated. I hoped that one day they might be able to help me in my schooling too.

I also learned something that week in summer camp that I would never forget, something that, I think, was a true turning point in my life. The camp that summer had a theme: "Make everything known to God." At first, this didn't seem to mean much to me. But then the priest explained that so many of us are alone in carrying the burden of our worries, thinking that nobody can help.

Whatever our problems are, whatever desires we carry, he told us, we should make it known to God, pray to Him, and trust that we are not alone. The priest told us to stop worrying, that it wasn't helpful to worry. What we needed to learn was to trust, and in order to trust, we needed to acknowledge what was true for us and make that known to God. After hearing the priest, I went to him. "I have something I want God to know," I said. "I want to be educated and to become a nurse." And the priest laid his hands on me, and in silence we prayed together. "I am so worried, God," I prayed. "I am so worried that I am too old and too poor to become a nurse. I am so worried that I will never live my dream. Please help me." And as I was praying this way, I felt a burden being lifted from my shoulders. Just by acknowledging my worry, I felt a great deal of it breaking away from me. It was as if all of a sudden I wasn't alone anymore in my fears and with my dream. I felt so relieved. From that day on, I made it a practice to let God know any concern I had—and to let go of it. Indeed, there was no use in worrying.

My conversion was very beneficial for me for practical reasons, but also because it gave me direction and guidance, a structure within which I could orient myself. Today, I think it may not matter all that much what religion one adheres to, but particularly for a young person it is very helpful to have some belief that supports her in finding her path.

When I came home, I told my dad that I was a Christian. He went very quiet. He had taught me that when you know you don't fully understand something, it's best to think about it before talking. So he said, "Please let me think about this." We didn't discuss the matter much more, and he never tried to talk me out of it. Many years later, he converted to Christianity himself.

During my time in Port Shepstone, I learned about a boarding school that was run by Swedish missionaries. It was a huge school that drew students from areas as far away as Durban and even Johannesburg. It was the only place in the area where students could stay to attend high school, so I decided this would be my chance. I asked Ms. McKechnie for assistance. Just as I had hoped for many years, she agreed to help me with my education. She made arrangements with the missionaries for me to receive room and board in exchange for work: cleaning, laundry, ironing, and helping with the younger children. Ms. McKechnie also secured a loan on my behalf from a distant cousin of mine so I could pay the tuition.

This time, however, I didn't have to run away from home. My father didn't like to see me leave him, but he also didn't try to hold me back. I think he had finally realized I had to follow my heart.

Every morning at school I got up around 5:00, tidied up the bedrooms, and then walked over to the younger children's area. I would help them get ready, pack their books, and make sure they had something to eat before leaving. In the evening, I again checked on them, bathed them, and got them ready for bed. Then I went back and collected all the tiny pieces of soap that the little ones had lost, put them in a can, and carried them over to the kitchen. "Can you please boil these for me?" I'd ask the kitchen people. Then I'd let the pieces of soap dry and cut them in neat little pieces. Every morning, at least one little child would come to me and say, "Auntie, do you have a piece of soap for me?" I was always so happy when I could help.

I made a little money on the side by repairing shoes for the children at the boarding school and also for people in the neighborhood. It was easy because all I needed was a leather needle and thread (which I would strengthen by soaking in wax). Soon I became pretty adept at repairing all kinds of shoes.

In some ways, I was a bit of an outcast in high school. Not that anybody shunned me or that there was any animosity. I was just quite a bit older than nearly all of the other students and I had very different interests. Most of the girls were interested in boys, and most of the boys were interested in girls. They would giggle, exchange little messages, go to parties, and so on—in short, the things teenagers like to do. For me, it was a bit different. I had a dream of becoming a nurse, and I was determined not to let myself get distracted. When boys came to ask me out, I would shoo them away: "Do you know how old I am? I could be your mother. Go and find somebody younger." Besides, I was busy studying, cleaning, taking care of the children, repairing shoes— there was never much room for idle time. Eventually, pretty much all of my classmates got married and that was that. I had decided that that was not my path. By then, I had grown used to being a bit of an outsider and it didn't bother me.

The principal, Mr. Mavundla, was a kind man who noticed that some of the kids occasionally teased me for being older and poorer than they were. He offered to help, but of course I would never tell on any of the children. He did, however, help me once, and for that I was thankful. High school graduation was a big social event, and in preparation, some of my classmates were pressuring me to accompany them to dance lessons and to choose a partner for that day. When I told them I couldn't go because I had a summer job as a cook at the Sunday school convention, they went to the principal to complain. But Mr. Mavundla told them that unlike them, I really needed the money and that they should leave me alone.

As in previous years, my father found an excuse not to attend the graduation ceremony. Still, it was a milestone for me, and when I finally made it through high school, I was proud and happy. I was twenty-eight, and once again I knew: I had made it this far, there was no way I would give up now.

Finding a nursing school turned out to be surprisingly easy. I applied to three hospitals—one in Victoria, one in Johannesburg, and one in Pietermaritzburg—and all three accepted me. I told my dad I wanted to go to Victoria, which is in Eastern Cape. He objected: "Oh no, you won't do that. I am from Eastern Cape, I know the people there. You will marry and never come back." So, reluctantly I told him I wouldn't go there and would instead go to Johannesburg. He was outraged: "My father went to Jo'burg and died in the mines, and I went to Jo'burg and came back a cripple. No, no, you will not go there." So I sent out letters saying I couldn't come.

By then, I'd figured out that whatever my choice, my father was going to object to it. I had to be smart about it. So I told him that I had been called to the magistrate's office, and that I'd been reprimanded for having turned down two government hospitals. It looked really bad. If I didn't start another position immediately, the government would likely remove my father's pension and I might even face jail time. Fortunately, however, our prayers had been heard, how very lucky we were! A third hospital had accepted me, one that was even close by, Edendale in Pietermaritzburg. It was our only chance. What could he say?

I remember my first day. Since I was a young teenager I'd been waiting for this. I had rebelled against my father and I had been laughed at by my teachers. I had run away from home and forgone marriage. I had worked so hard, and now I was finally here. This was it, my dream was materializing—I was becoming a nurse! It was a very happy day.

It was 1964, and Edendale was a new hospital, not even ten years old. It had room for several hundred patients, and being the only hospital in the district, it served a huge area. Many people suffered from problems resulting from malnutrition, particularly children who came in with hugely swollen bellies and empty eyes. There was also a lot of tuberculosis, a disease that back then was often misdiagnosed and misunderstood. When people noticed the symptoms, they would usually go to the traditional healers, but these healers didn't have any help to offer. By the time patients decided to come to the hospital, they were often in a very late stage. There were many tests to our courage.

We students lived in a dorm; I shared my room with seven fellow nursing students. The second year, there were only four of us in a room, and from the third year on I had a room to myself. None of that mattered much though—I would have stayed with seven in the room the whole time. I was just so happy that I was becoming a nurse.

By the time I entered nursing school, I was used to playing the role of an "auntie." For many years now, I had been quite a bit older than most of my classmates, and so I had naturally grown to take care of them. This kind of relationship didn't change in nursing school. I would braid hair, help with studying, give advice. I was just "Auntie Abe."

Our curriculum included both college classes and hospital work, and it covered preventative, curative, and tertiary care. We had what we called a "block" of classes, say for two or three months, and then a block of maybe four or five months in the ward. I appreciated this system because it ensured that we would immediately put into practice what we had learned. The studying part was interesting for me, but working with patients was truly amazing. I got so much love from them, so many kind words! Sometimes when I arrived at my ward, patients would be waiting for me, asking, "Can you please give me my injection?" or "Can you please give me my bath?" "But wasn't there another nurse here earlier?" I'd say. "Yes, Sister," I often heard, "but I wanted it to be you." People were so kind and grateful. Even the doctors were very appreciative of me and used every occasion to let me know.

It was an excellent school. Teachers were very engaged and would answer questions and offer help even after hours. We often studied in groups where the students supported one another and the trainers supervised our practical work.

Occasionally, I had some friction with other nurses, however. I think they felt I was overzealous. "Oh, who do you think you are? You want to be like Florence Nightingale?" they would say. I didn't know how to respond. The truth was that yes, I deeply admired Florence Nightingale, though I would have never dared to compare myself to her. I just wanted to help. I couldn't understand how a nurse could leave her ward to have a cigarette if there were still patients needing her. I just wanted to help, that was all.

During those years I didn't have much contact with my father. There was so much to do. Fortunately, as nurses-in-training, we were being paid. Not only could I immediately start repaying the cousin who had been kind enough to give me a loan for my high school tuition, I could also send money to my dad. I would always write a letter and send it along with the money, but he never responded. I think he was hurt because he was missing me so badly and it was hard for him to live without me.

A couple of years later, however, after he'd converted to Christianity, he held a big celebration for our entire community. An ox was slaughtered, people played music, and the entire village came. My dad announced that he had to say something. Now this was unusual because he was not a man of big words and he was not used to addressing a crowd of people. There were two things he needed to say and two reasons for this celebration, he told us. He wanted to say "thank you" and he wanted to say "sorry." The "thank you" was to the head man and to the community for having helped him through difficult times, and "sorry" was to his daughter Abe, because he'd always tried to prevent her from fulfilling her dream. He said he was very proud of me for achieving it.

And it certainly had been an unexpected road for many who'd known me as a child. Soon after I had completed my general nursing diploma, I'd had an interesting encounter. I was walking down the corridor in my ward when I happened to meet a man whom I immediately recognized. He looked at me. "I seem to know this face," he said. "You look like somebody I know." "No," I replied. "I don't look like somebody you know, I am that somebody," and I showed him my ID. "It can't be! It can't be!" he stammered. "You can't be a nurse, I don't believe it, it's amazing!" I told him,

"Well, when I was a first-grader and you asked us what we wanted to be, you laughed at me when I told you. And here we are, and I am a nurse now." He did not know what to say.

3

Hands to Hold

I was thirty-two and just shy of three years into nursing school when something unexpected happened: I fell in love with a child.

The little girl was only a few months old, a beautiful mix of an Indian mother and a black South African father. The poor little one was an outcast before she could even walk. The father had become mentally ill after the girl's birth and started horribly abusing his wife. Being Indian, the girl's mother wanted to go back to the colored section of town, but with a black child that was not allowed. So the mother left the girl with her paternal grandparents. Most unfortunately, however, the grandmother died soon after and the grandfather married another woman who didn't want anything to do with a mixed child. So the grandfather gave the child to a cousin who took her in but begrudgingly, because he thought it would be much harder for his own daughter to find a husband with this child around. That's when I saw the baby.

I called her Zuzu. In full, her name is Nonzuzo, which means "mother of reward." Seeing this beautiful little girl,

I just couldn't bear the thought of her living in a house where she was neither wanted nor loved. So I talked to everybody—the grandfather, the cousin, the *inkosi*, or head man—and everybody happily agreed to my adopting the child.

Little did I realize that this was just the beginning of a force that would shape the rest of my life. Zuzu was a beautiful gift life offered to me. She was the first of more than twenty children I would adopt over the next few decades.

By the time Zuzu came along, I had given up on the idea of ever getting married—who would marry somebody my age? Besides, I saw my life's task to be helping the poor, the sick, children, and the elderly—in giving to the community. That was my love and my passion. Marriage was no longer a consideration—and with that, the option of having my own children also vanished.

But Zuzu was my child. Every single child I ever adopted, I fell in love with; every one is truly my child.

Since I was studying and working at the hospital and still living in a dorm, I asked my sister-in-law if Zuzu could live with her for the first years, and she kindly took her in. Fortunately, I now earned enough money so that I was able to pay for what the child needed. I was registered as the child's mother and spent time with her whenever I could. After I finished my general nursing degree, I was able to take Zuzu to live with me full-time.

Having a child in my life made me realize that a general nursing degree alone would not suffice for me to serve in the way I wanted. I had always loved babies, and so naturally I was drawn to pediatrics. Zuzu simply intensified that longing. So I applied for a position at Victoria Hospital in Eastern Cape, where I knew I could take classes in that field. I worked there for a few years and became a pediatric nurse, then went back to Pietermaritzburg.

In the meantime, I had adopted another child, my son Hopeson. Oh, how adorable he was! And like with all of my children, the poor little boy was in a dire situation when I met him. His mother was an alcoholic, his father unknown. One day, the mother dropped him off at the place next door, telling my neighbor she was going to the market. She never came back. I talked to the neighbor, I talked to Social Security, and I talked to the inkosi—what a mess! It was so sad to see the little boy getting dumped over and over. No one wanted the responsibility. In the end, I took him in and adopted him, and now Zuzu and Hopeson would grow up as brother and sister. From here on out, I started adopting children whenever I found one in need. If you see a little child suffering, how can you ignore it? More and more children joined me, and with them more and more love came to me.

I made good money as a nurse, but at times, I was living with ten or fifteen children in one room. They all needed food, clothing, and schooling. Plus, I had my father to take care of and my brother's children (my brother was not doing well), and there was our little house to maintain. It was a busy time.

Seeing my first children approaching adolescence, I thought it would be beneficial if I knew more about psychology. My hope was to understand them better and help as best as I could when they would face psychological issues as teenagers. Of course, I also realized that study in this field was likely to help me in dealing with the many sufferings of our communities. So I went to a psychiatric clinic in Newcastle, about 250 kilometers from Pietermaritzburg, where I earned additional qualifications as a psychiatric nurse. This was not atypical for me: my interests are usually sparked by some problem at hand, some issue that I need to address, and the way I go about addressing those is through education. When I started having eye problems a few years later, I became interested in ophthalmology and received training as an ophthalmological nurse outside Pretoria, close to the border of Zimbabwe. All of these additional qualifications would later prove to be great assets in what was to become the most challenging time in my life.

Over the years while working in different hospitals, I was frequently urged to go out into the country and provide medical services to those who didn't have access to hospitals or doctors. "Abe," I heard again and again, "you are a community person. You always wanted to be there for communities and not just individuals. Go to where you are needed most." I certainly liked the idea of working more closely with a community. In the hospital, we might see a patient for only a few days, weeks at most, before they'd be discharged.

In some ways I felt I could be much more effective if I saw people in their own environments. Without that, even advice as simple and sound as "Try to wash every day" is often wasted. If a woman comes from a rural area without access to water, she may have a very hard time getting enough water to even drink; washing every day is out of the question. Knowing her situation would help a nurse give better advice. Plus, for many people in these outlying communities at that time, if you didn't go to them, they virtually had no way of ever seeing a medically trained professional. Remote villages didn't have (and many still don't have) streets, much less cars to drive to a city. Patients from these areas who could still walk would often have to hike for two or three days to come to a town with a hospital. And for those who were elderly or seriously ill, this was not an option. Even if a village had dirt roads, and a sort of minibus system was available, many people couldn't afford to pay for the bus. There were so many who were in dire need.

The Methodist Mission ran a couple of hospitals providing services for people in remote areas. When I started with them in 1974, we were targeting northern Zululand, the region bordering Mozambique. It was a huge area, and its roads were very bad, so usually we would take a small one-engine plane to get into the valleys.

The terrain was so rugged that it was often hard to see houses or villages because they were hidden underneath the shrubbery and trees. They were mostly small farming communities where people would barter with each other; money was practically unknown. Few places had electricity or even running water. Most people lived with extended families, and family planning was virtually unknown, so it was not uncommon for couples to have ten or more children. Those farmers who happened to have enough produce to possibly sell in the bigger towns or cities had to overcome the limitations of a poor infrastructure. Even if they were lucky enough to have a bus service nearby, the bus would run only once or twice a day.

The medical situation there was desperate. Leprosy was common, typhoid rampant. Poverty was pervasive, so in many areas people were starving. In their desperation, they would grind up a certain bark. A teaspoon for an adult, a pinch for a child would make them not feel the hunger for an entire day. That, of course, caused all kinds of intestinal obstructions. Children and adults alike were lying in dilapidated huts, unable to move, with their bellies swollen. The most basic sanitation was lacking. It was so sad! The traditional healers could help with some diseases, but they were powerless against most of them, especially epidemics. The situation was further worsened by a lot of superstition and ignorance. Many pregnant women died during delivery because they were given a certain bark at the wrong time. So much suffering!

However, as severe as the medical and economic situation was, the people's spirits were left unbroken. Far from being hardened by their circumstances, they often showed a tremendous amount of kindness, helping each other wherever they could. I would even encounter a great sense of joy. Women who came to the mission clinics frequently had to walk all day to get there, sometimes with two children on their backs. They would arrive exhausted and dehydrated, and yet, there was a gratitude in them that was astonishing. There were no secrets; people talked openly and freely. What a loving community!

So we'd fly out to these remote areas in our little mission plane and start working wherever we could find an appropriate spot. We administered medicine, gave drops, alerted doctors to some patients, and flew out other patients who were more critical.

As we went out to do our work, the pilot of the plane was very mischievous with me. He knew I was afraid of flying, and one day as we were taking off, I noticed that he was going an unusual route. "I need to fly over my house and wave to my wife," he explained. "I have a bad feeling we might not come back, so I need to say good-bye to her." For a short moment, I believed him, but when I saw his mocking face, I started laughing. The two of us had a lot of fun on our flights.

My work with mobile services in northern Zululand was an eye-opening experience. I now truly understood the need for a medical presence in the communities. I'd already sensed it when I was in the hospital. There I would often see three to four hundred people a day! It was very exhausting. We needed to see people near their homes, enable locals to take on certain tasks, and help people to help themselves. We had to devise an educational system that could sustain itself and provide a basis for much larger outreach. Otherwise, no matter how hard we worked, there would always be more than we could possibly handle.

So I sat down with a doctor and we thought up a plan for how to draw from the local resources. Traditionally, women were already assisting with baby deliveries, so why not see if we could reach out and train them further? So I went to the induna, a high-ranking representative, and asked if he could organize a meeting with representatives of all five tribal wards. A tribal ward typically has an induna, an inkosi, and council members that represent some fifty families. He said he'd try, but people were a bit suspicious. "Sister Abe, you work for the government and people are afraid that you are here because they are using illegal herbs." I assured him that I wasn't there to set anybody up. On the contrary, I wanted to see how we could all work together to better the conditions during childbirth.

The meeting was a moderate success. The women were still a bit suspicious, but at least some were willing to see what we had to offer. It also helped that I was curious to understand their methods and see how we could best integrate them. So we all came together, and they showed us what they did, and then the doctor and I developed a curriculum designed to improve on the current process. I talked to the mission, and they were willing to support the idea and provide us with the necessary facilities. So we set up a two-month training program that covered all the basics for training of TBAs, Traditional Birth Attendants. For example, I had a group of trainees accompany me for one week in the maternity ward, and then they'd go home for one week to practice what they had learned. Then they would come back for the next week and participate in a different ward, and so on.

Women came from all over the area, and we always had more people willing than we could accommodate. I would also go to the traditional healers and ask them specifically to join the program. They were the ones who commonly delivered children and such, so it was very beneficial to have them on board. For two months they would live in the mission before going off to their communities. Of course, many of the women couldn't read or write, so I created visual aids for them to learn from, and I also set up study groups where at least one person was literate and could read to the others. It was a very successful program that educated hundreds of women. Since these women were already known by their community, it was easier for them to be accepted there, and their new skills gained them a lot of respect.

We soon realized, however, that many of the women we trained would leave when they found a job that would pay some money or when their families wanted them back. It became clear that if we were to retain them, we would need to offer a small stipend. I talked to the Methodist Mission, and fortunately they were willing to help out. With the aid of a stipend system and a refined selection process, more and more women were able to stay with the program.

This process was my first experience with building a true community organization around medical needs. I could see that it was one thing to assist somebody with a delivery, another thing to train a local woman who would then be qualified to help hundreds of women to deliver. Later in my life I would build many more community organizations.

Ms. McKechnie had taught me a long time ago that in order to help others, I needed two things: I needed to be able to help myself, and I needed skills. I now understood that this was not only true for individuals but also for communities. The more skills and knowledge a community had, the better equipped it was to help itself. As a child I had grown up with ubuntu— the idea that an individual is a person only inasmuch as she is part of a community. I believed that only as a community would we be able to rise above the problems. Soon enough that concept was to be put to the ultimate test, as South Africa was about to be hit by a pandemic so vast and tragic that it was completely unprepared to handle it: AIDS.

By the mid-1970s, we had built up a wonderful organization of Traditional Birth Attendants who were willing and able to provide the assistance their communities so desperately needed. They could make basic diagnoses, administer medications, write referrals, and help out with many other needs. Finally, we had at least a rudimentary medical structure in place.

On a more personal note, by the time I had left for northern Zululand, I had already adopted four children. Of course, I could not take them with me to the mission, so my sister was kind enough to take them in. I sent her money for their needs, and she took care of them. It wasn't a bad arrangement, but over time I missed my children more and more. Normally I wouldn't get much more than one weekend a month to see them, and while my arrival brought many smiles, my departures were always difficult. "Gogo, why do you have to leave again?" they would ask, and my heart would grow heavy. I understood the situation wasn't fair to them.

In April 1976, I learned that the Department of Health was looking for a nurse to provide mobile services out of Greytown in KwaZulu-Natal. It was another remote area, and my task would be to drive around in a van and provide medical services to outlying communities.

I jumped at the chance, mainly because it allowed me to be much closer to my children. Greytown was less than three hours from Harding, which meant that I would be able to see my children every weekend, maybe even during the week. I also felt the position was appropriate for me, as by this time I had quite a bit of experience in the field. So I got myself an old car and moved to a township in Greytown. Townships offered inexpensive government housing to working-class people, and so during the week I lived in one of these small houses.

Every workday, I would leave the house around 7:30 a.m. and come back around 7:00 p.m. I would take a government van that was specially equipped for medical missions. On site, I'd set up a little tent that provided shelter for those waiting in line; inside, there was a little table for consultation, shelves stacked with medicine, and a sink for hand washing. Sometimes the farmers would allow me to use their garages, which gave me a bit more space.

Usually I had three or four medical service stops per day, meaning I would drive out to a farm or a village, set up my tent, and work for a couple of hours before moving on to the next stop. People in need knew my schedule because I would call the evening before to confirm my next day's arrival.

The only real hardship I had was the weather. Heavy rainstorms often visit that area of the country, so my van would sometimes get stuck in the mud. Whenever that happened, I would call the farmers and tell them, "I am here to help your workers. It is in your best interest to maintain their good health, no? So please come and help me, I am stuck." Usually, that logic made sense, and the farmer would send somebody to help out.

During the weekends, I was now free to spend time with my children. I was so happy! Usually, I would go home Friday evening and then leave early in the morning on Monday. When I arrived, the children would all jump up and down for joy and we would hug each other. Zuzu was the type who would cry when she was excited, and I remember her crying and crying when I came home. I would ask her, "Why are you crying?" and she would say, "Because I am so happy, Ma!"

The house in Harding had only one room, so we would play games until it was time for all of us to go to sleep together. In the morning, they'd take a bath while I fixed them breakfast. Afterward we would head to town to do some shopping; there we would buy the necessary things for the household—clothing, food, and such—but of course I would always get the children something small that was just for fun.

Greytown had a fairly sophisticated hospital, but it offered no real outreach into the rural communities, and so even the people in my township were reluctant to go there. This changed when I moved there. Neighbors soon realized what I was doing and came to see me. Often when I came back from the rural areas, there would already be a line of people outside my house waiting for me. They would bring me their children and ask for advice. They trusted me enough so that when I recommended they see a doctor in the hospital, they would overcome their apprehension and do as advised. Because of my contact with many people there, I soon developed a lot of good friendships in the area.

After a while, I noticed that some of the women there had a drinking problem. When I talked to them I realized that many of them were simply lonely and didn't have anybody to talk to. So I started a Ladies

Club on Thursday evenings. We didn't have any particular agenda—just to meet. Some would bring their
knitting with them; others would prepare food. It was
all rather casual, and the idea was that the women could
talk freely—and confidentially—about what was worrying them. Soon the group took on a life of its own,
and the women began to meet on Saturdays as well. It
was really lovely to see it grow.

The youngsters didn't seem to have much of a social
life either, so I suggested we start a choir. The local
Anglican church supported the idea and gave us a little
room where we could practice together. Soon, we had
some forty, fifty teenagers—a group so big that we had
to divide them into smaller groups. We practiced cho-
ral arrangements as well as wedding and funeral music.
They sang so beautifully! After only a few months we
started giving concerts, and people liked them so much
that the group was asked to sing in the surrounding
communities. When I left Greytown a few years later,
the choir gave me a wonderful farewell concert and
even followed me to my new location and sang in the
local church for me. It was very moving.

Of course, there were adversities as well. It was a
fairly crime-ridden area, so I wasn't surprised when one
day I came home to find that my place had been bro-
ken into and my cassette player had been stolen. A few
days later, in the middle of the night, I heard a ruckus
outside. I got up and cautiously opened the door and
saw that my car had been jacked up and all the tires had
been taken off. But to my surprise, the tires, lug nuts,

and everything were still lying next to it with no thief to be seen. I didn't know what to make of it.

The following week, a teenager was waiting for me at my gate. I asked him what I could do for him, but he didn't want to talk. The next few days he returned, and eventually he told me he'd a confession to make. He'd been a member of a group that someone was paying to go around stealing and as such had been involved in the recent incidents at my house. He said he was very sorry but it wasn't in his power to give me back the cassette player. "Don't worry," I told him, "it doesn't matter. But I have a question for you: why is it that you left the tires after you took them off my car?" He looked at me with big eyes and said, "Because we were scared. We had nearly finished when we saw two big white army men with guns coming out of your place. They were after us, so we all ran away." Now, that was very strange as I knew there hadn't been any men in my place that night (or any other night). "Are you sure?" I said. "We all saw them, I swear," he replied. I didn't say anything but thought to myself, Well, clearly they had a vision that was brought to them in order to protect me!

I stayed in Greytown for four years. During that time, the acceptance of the hospital grew, and the mobile service established the necessary link between the rural areas and the medical community. I felt very much at ease in my neighborhood, and I loved my friends and my patients dearly, but I also began to feel that I could be more useful in areas where medical services were less developed.

At the beginning of 1980, I heard of another struggling area in KwaZulu-Natal—the region of Underberg. Underberg wasn't so far from Greytown, only about two hundred kilometers, but it bordered Lesotho, and the remote valleys in this mountainous area were completely underserved. The nearest hospital was in Pietermaritzburg, at least one hundred kilometers away, and the mountain tribes living in the region didn't have the means to make their way to Underberg, much less to a hospital that far away. Though there were basic dirt roads in place, virtually no one could afford a car, and even the small amount of money required to take a shared bus was more than people could afford.

I was told the area was suffering badly from leprosy, tuberculosis, and tetanus. Immunization was practically unknown. Western medicine was often shunned due to superstition and even further discouraged by local power structures. To help alleviate some of the problems, a center in Underberg was due to open with a mobile service established for the surrounding area. The problem was that none of the nurses wanted to go there. Underberg was just, as they put it, "outside of everything." There was really nothing going on—no amenities, shops, entertainment, anything. The nurses who were married didn't want to leave their husbands to move to such an area, and the younger ones were afraid they would lose their boyfriends. So my boss, Mrs. Strydom, approached me and said, "You are old enough, you don't need these kinds of things, why don't you go?" She was right; I didn't need these things. So I decided to drive to Underberg and see for myself. I met with a few ladies who belonged to the local farmers' association, and I told them if they could provide me with housing, I would give it a try. Initially it was meant to be a temporary assignment, just for three months.

Soon the arrangements were made and I moved into a small house with two rooms plus a bathroom and a kitchen. One of the rooms was my bedroom and living area; the other room was the clinic. In the beginning, there wasn't much furniture. I remember how the first woman I helped deliver a baby did so on the small bench in my kitchen. Her name was Lindo; she was a lovely fifteen-year-old who had walked the better part of the day to receive help for the birth. So despite the fact that my setup was rudimentary, I was happy with it and felt I could do good work there.

I quickly realized that the medical conditions in the area were even more desperate than I had imagined. There were two general practitioners; one of them was already retired and the other one was so overworked that he would simply close his office and go for a vacation when he felt he needed to, leaving the people there with nowhere to turn. Neither doctor had set foot in some of the remoter areas of the region, and as a result, not only did I find leprosy, TB, and tetanus, but there was also polio and a whole barrage of other diseases. It was particularly heartbreaking to see how many children were suffering from diseases that could have been

prevented through shots. Hygiene was a huge problem, many people looked malnourished, and there were
also no antibiotics, so people died from what began as
simple infections.

To make matters more complicated, when I first
arrived in Underberg, there was a lot of resistance to my
assignment by the white community. They weren't bad
people, they were just not used to the idea of a black
nurse. I remember when I arrived with Mrs. Strydom,
the farmers' wives immediately petitioned for me to
be replaced by a white nurse. When they realized that
wasn't going to happen, they reluctantly settled for
coping with "that black nurse" for three months, hop-
ing that would give Mrs. Strydom enough time to find
a white one. When Mrs. Strydom left, she shook her
head. "Oh, Abe," she said. "What are you going to do?
I am leaving you in such a mess. I don't know how
you are going to manage." I told her not to worry,
that things would improve. "I will make them like
me," I said. "I will leave them no choice!" I don't think
Mrs. Strydom was quite convinced though.

First, I sat down with the farmers' wives. I told them
I needed help because I didn't know the area and I
asked them how I could best assist them. My boss had
told me to set up mobile services on the farms, but
I knew the people from the really remote settlements
had no means of getting to the farms. So instead, the
farmers' wives and I mapped out the area, setting up an
itinerary of where I would be each day so people would
know how to reach me.

In the beginning, it was nearly overwhelming; there was so much to do! I didn't have a problem acquiring all the medicine I needed for the vaccinations and immunizations, but there were so many people who needed them, sometimes I thought the lines would never end. How could I possibly do this?

It is a great help that I never required much sleep. Whenever I felt too exhausted to carry on, I would take a quick nap—a couple of minutes here or there. That's all I needed, and that was very lucky, because it meant I could work until late or even through the night. We didn't have electricity, but often the farmers from the area were kind enough to help out. Those with cars would come after sunset, form a circle with the cars, and turn on the headlamps, providing enough light to continue taking patients. In my previous assignment, I'd had the weekends off to spend time with my children and do some gardening. But now, there were no more weekends; I always worked. The first month I had four hundred patients, the second month eight hundred, the third month three thousand. When I submitted my statistics, Mrs. Strydom couldn't believe it. "This is impossible," she said. I told her, "Please come here and see for yourself." She came and stayed with me and watched me work until 2:00 a.m. Then she said, "I am exhausted. Can we go home?" I said, "People from the remote areas have walked a day or two with their children to see us. How can we go to sleep?"

Though I spent all of my waking hours helping the community, my standing with the white members improved only slowly. Many of them realized the benefits of having a nurse in town, but for some, it was difficult to get over the race barrier. In order to reach out to the white farmers, I had started to go from farm to farm to talk to them. "I am a nurse from the Department of Health, and I want to discuss with you how we can help you best." One day I had an appointment with a farmer's wife at 9:00 a.m. I was fifteen minutes early and she wasn't there, so I waited until around five past nine, when she drove up with a pickup truck full of dogs—small ones, big ones, all sorts. They went straight for me and bit my legs and ripped my skirt and my petticoat until I was in panties. They bit every spot they could get to. Fortunately, when I am in shock, I don't run, I freeze. If I had run they might have killed me. But since I just stood still, eventually the farmer's wife came over and got the dogs off me. On her way over, she stumbled, and I think that made her even angrier, because she yelled at me that the situation was entirely my fault. I didn't object. Eventually she came to her senses and offered to buy me a new uniform, but I told her it wasn't necessary.

The next day I was so bitten and bruised that I had to call Mrs. Strydom and ask for a temporary sub who could run the clinic for me. I spent two weeks in Harding recovering, during which I had a lot of time to reflect on what had happened. At first, I was angry with the farmer's wife, and then I was angry with myself, and then I noticed how both kinds of anger fed off each other, and I thought, This isn't helping anybody.

After all, the incident didn't have a large impact on my life. In short, I let go. Mrs. Strydom encouraged me to report the woman to the police, but that would have only made things worse. So I did nothing against her. When I happened to meet her a couple of weeks later, she said that her husband had insisted she buy me new clothes and asked what I needed. Again, I told her that this wasn't necessary. "There is nothing to worry about, I have another skirt," I assured her. And really, there was nothing to worry about. You see, I think her husband had already scolded her, and words can hurt even more than physical pain. Why add to the situation? So I forgave her, and she never gave me a hard time again. In fact, she was friendly after that. It was a horrible experience but one that taught me that at the end of the day, it's much easier to understand, to forgive, and to let go.

Little by little, the white community lost their apprehension toward me. They started letting me immunize their children and began helping me more with my outreach. Eventually they even invited me to their dinners and to give talks in the classrooms. It was really a rather loving group; they just had to get used to me.

My strategy was and still is to try to meet the people where they are in their lives and accept them. There is little hope of improving our relationships if we begin by assigning blame. I just refused to play into the racist game. There was so much hurt on each side, I knew somebody had to make the first step. Once I understood that, it really was quite easy.

Another big step in racial relations was integration in the churches. When I came to the area, Christianity was considered a religion for white people. Regardless of the denomination, only white people attended church. I felt this was very unfortunate, as I had been lucky enough to experience firsthand the benefits of religion, and it pained me to see so many people being excluded for racial reasons. Of course, this was still the time of Apartheid, so people were used to segregation, but I wasn't willing to accept the status quo. I tried to convince people it was OK for them to attend church. "But Abe," they would say, "our boss has told us not to worship there with him." "In church," I would reply, "he is not your boss anymore, he is just another member of the church community, just as you are. Come, let's go together." So I would start taking people into the churches. It didn't matter to me what church. On Sunday morning, I would start with the Roman Catholic church from 6:00 to 7:00 a.m., I would go to the Anglican church from 7:30 to 9:00, and then at 11:00 I would attend the Congregational church. Every time, I would take as many people with me as were interested in joining. "It's just in our heads," I would tell them. "Let's not carry an Apartheid mentality into church. We'll just go, and sooner or later everybody will embrace the idea that race doesn't matter to God."

Oh, how people stared at us in disbelief. One day I entered a church and a man approached me, and, assuming I must be a maid, he asked me with a stern voice whom I was working for. This, of course, was meant to convey the threat that he would tell my boss about my insolence. I told him I was a nurse and that I wasn't working for one person but for everybody. To that he didn't know how to respond.

The white community didn't like that we were disturbing the status quo. But equally if not more problematic was the mental barrier of many black people. Some felt they didn't have the right to go to church and feared repercussions; many, however, simply carried an Apartheid mentality that cast "them" against "us."

Fortunately, there are always those who won't give in to fear or prejudice. Gradually, we started getting more and more encouraging smiles when we entered a church. Often a row of people would open up to make room for us. Eventually, the white people from church would invite the black people to join them for tea afterward. Initially the black people still thought of themselves as servants and had a hard time with it. But I told them, "We are all together here and we should cultivate fellowship. It's good for all of us." Over time, they overcame their apprehensions. Really, all it took was time. People needed time to get used to the idea, and slowly their resistance melted away.

The priests were supportive of the process and joined us in our efforts. Encouraged, I began to engage even more, particularly with the Anglican church. I helped the priests translate into Zulu, and I also conducted weddings, funerals, and sometimes even a service. Before I held a service, the priest would give the mass and hold Holy Communion, but after a while I would do those too when the priest wasn't available. A number of years later, in 1989, I completed training to officially become an Anglican lay minister. When Bishop Michael Nuttall licensed me, he asked me to become a full-time priest, but I told him I didn't have time for that. Still, I was happy to be certified to lead a congregation.

By that time, it seemed to me that no one had any difficulty with a black woman preacher. Of course, I would sometimes be mocked for my accent and my English, but I liked it when people corrected me because it gave me a chance to learn. But the racial tensions had all but vanished, and it seemed no one looked back. It was really quite beautiful.

I often hear people saying that "people are people," that we will never change. But that is not my experience. We may need a little push sometimes, and we may all need some time to adjust to change, but I am very hopeful that eventually we will all learn from one another and move forward together as one community. Apartheid had brought about terrible divisions in South Africa, and I knew we had to overcome great barriers in our heads to truly fit together as one community. But we did it—and what better place than in church?

About five months after I began my position, when Mrs. Strydom came to check on me, nobody asked to replace me with a white nurse anymore. On the contrary, Mrs. Strydom told me that a number of people had approached her to please encourage me to stay. Even now, thirty years later, it still makes me smile. I am still in Underberg, and I would like to think that we are now one big community.

One of my first challenges, beyond changing people's mind-sets, was to commandeer the necessary resources. When I arrived in Underberg, there were precious few that I could leverage. As luck had it though, I happen to be very short, and short people—women in particular—are said to be very stubborn. I don't know if this is always true, but in my case it certainly is. Whenever I needed something—a tent to receive patients in, a particular medicine, anything really—I would relentlessly hound my supervisor from the Department of Health until I got it. Soon I did not lack equipment or medical provisions. More difficult, however, was finding the people I needed to put programs into place. To make everything work, locals were required to cooperate and take over some tasks. Back in northern Zululand I'd had good experience with approaching the traditional healers, so I thought I would try that in Underberg. Initially, that met with a lot of resistance, so I called for a meeting. "Why can't we all get together and discuss how to best support each other?" I said. They were very apprehensive, and when they finally agreed to get together, they came only to tell me they had no interest in collaboration. "Western medicine looks down on us," they said. "Why would we work with you? We have helped people for hundreds of years, but you just ignore us and disregard our methods." Well, I could understand their perspective. It would take a while to gain their trust.

Over the next few months I tried to reach out to them as much as possible. I spent time with them individually as well as in groups, and more and more I came to appreciate what they had to offer. Yes, there was a lot of superstition, and yes, their skills often couldn't help when it came to certain diseases such as TB. However, the healers were extremely skillful and knowledgeable in other areas—for example, in psychotherapy and dealing with trauma. Years earlier, I had completed a certificate as a psychiatric nurse, but to observe these healers work with their patients was just amazing.

I remember one girl, no older than twelve or thirteen, who had a series of psychotic breakdowns. Her parents had died years earlier, and her aunt and uncle were raising her. She started having seizures of some form, and her body would twist in convulsions while she screamed and screamed; nothing could make her stop. When the attack was over, she would totally shut down, not looking at anybody or speaking a word for weeks at a time. I did not know what to do with her, and I had little hope that the hospital would be able to provide any help. So I sent her to a healer. Now, that man didn't know anything about her background, but he could tell right away that she was not with her parents, and that that's where the problem was rooted. I don't know what exactly he did—I think he had an animal slaughtered and he probably did something to connect with the dead parents—whatever it was, the girl opened up and started talking again, and over time she slowly yet fully recovered. It was just amazing to watch.

Healers were also able to show people practical methods to deal with common ailments and wounds—for instance, the trauma women experienced after delivering babies. They would tell them during the first few days after delivery to squat down in a certain way because that helped the alignment of the wound. For things of this nature, their advice worked well, and I learned a lot from them. In turn, the more I listened and acknowledged some of their methods, the more they were willing to study and understand what Western medicine had to offer. I also won their confidence by helping them with bureaucratic and legal matters, and by bringing them to gardens where they would learn, for example, how to debark a tree without killing it. Slowly our relationships improved and we started referring patients to each other, depending on the nature of the illness.

Collaborating with the traditional healers was a big step. Not only did it help ease both our patient loads, it also helped heal the rift that had separated us. The need for medical care was so great, we really needed to work together.

Still, with all of our efforts, it became clear we needed to build a far better medical system to support the area effectively. More medical personnel, a centralized mobile service system, and a better facility were required. In short, Underberg needed its own clinic.

After my first year, I started petitioning the Department of Health, telling them over and over, "You said I would have to see no more than three to four hundred patients a month, but the truth is that I am seeing ten times as many, and it's still not enough. I cannot do this alone; it is impossible. We need help here." So after much begging and pleading, dozens of letters and countless phone calls, they decided to send another person over to check on me. I think they still couldn't believe the numbers I had submitted were true.

A doctor from the provincial health department came on a Friday, the day I'd requested. We worked side by side, splitting the patients into two long queues. But even with two of us, the queues never seemed to get shorter. When evening approached, I told him I needed to leave by no later than 9:00 p.m., because I had to be with my children in Harding, and it was a three-hour drive. "But Sister Abe," he said, "there are still so many people waiting. Who will take care of your queue if you go?" "That's it, Doctor," I replied, "that is exactly it! There usually is one queue, and it never seems to end. It's just not possible for one person."

When he finally understood the situation, he grew pensive for a while and then said, "I now see. Please, can you draw up a blueprint of what you need here? I will then make a report, using your numbers and your drawing, and we'll see what we can do."

I was happy we seemed to be getting some traction and immediately contacted a farmer who I knew was good at drawing. I told him, "Please, just design a clinic that you would send your own children to." So he went about it, and when I met with him a few weeks later, he showed me a huge detailed sketch. It was so nicely done that I could submit it exactly as is.

Lo and behold, we got a new clinic approved, and once we had obtained permission, things went very quickly. I think they built it directly from the sketch we had submitted, using prefab walls and materials. In only three months, we had a clinic that even included an X-ray room and a maternity ward! That was in 1985.

Servicing our clients would be much easier with a permanent building, and there was another benefit: now that we had our own medical center, it was also easier to recruit nurses who were willing to work in this area. Soon, we had a staff of eight qualified medical practitioners. Before, we had only one mobile service; now we could afford to have three. We even got an ambulance—a vast improvement over transporting patients in the back of a truck.

In these first years in Underberg, much was accomplished. People worked together to create a stronger community and an improved medical system. The churches, the farmers, the laborers, the health department, and the social workers all contributed in one way or another. True, there was no shortage of problems that remained, but we were making progress—until a disease came that would ravage our country and change all of our lives.

4

The AIDS Crisis

A patient came to see me with what she thought was a cold. But her face didn't have the look of one with a cold, and I remember thinking, This is something else. I gave her some medicine and sent her back home, but I was worried. So, the next day I called up the farm she worked on. "How's your lady that works in the kitchen?" I asked the farmer. "Oh, she is not better," he replied. So I went to the farm to see her. She appeared even sicker than the day before, and I knew there wasn't anything more I could do for her, so I wrote her a referral letter for the hospital in Edendale. There, she was told that she had TB. Of course, TB is no laughing matter, so to ensure that she knew how to properly administer the necessary medication, I offered her a place to stay with me for a few days. While she was there, I noticed that she was developing a rash that looked similar to shingles but wasn't. It was a rash that I didn't like at all. When it began to spread over her back, I took her to another doctor. That doctor looked at her, and then he took me aside. "Sister," he said, "have you heard of the new disease they call AIDS? I think this might be it." I had heard some rumors about it. "Doesn't it come from monkeys?" I said. We sent the patient back to Edendale, and from there she was transferred to the Richmond hospital. About six months later, she came back and died almost immediately.

Even before she returned, however, I went to Edendale. If this was a new disease, I wanted to be prepared for it in the event of more cases. "If you have any training on this HIV and AIDS, please let me know and contact my boss," I told the doctors. Soon after, I attended the training program on AIDS, and then I began to notice more and more people displaying symptoms. At the time, there was little I could do, so I would send them to Edendale, where they'd eventually be discharged to come home and die. I was very worried about how rapidly this disease was spreading. Little did I know this was the beginning of a pandemic that was about to kill millions of people in South Africa alone.

From the beginning, AIDS carried a huge stigma in South Africa, a stigma that was based on misinformation and superstition. Many people thought it was a homosexual's disease and that infections would only occur in the gay community. Initially, some churches and even the government helped spread this rumor. This was terrible on many levels. It led to heterosexual people thinking they were safe, and, since homosexuality was considered shameful (and still is by many people here), this belief also prevented those who were already infected from coming forward for treatment out of fear of public exposure. People with HIV were not only stricken with a deadly disease, they were also blamed for it.

Others attributed the disease to witchcraft. This, of course, was equally unfortunate, because those people thought there was nothing they could do about it. Even worse, this particular notion gave rise to the suspicion that the witchcraft had been performed on behalf of some enemy. Then, of course, people would start looking for who that enemy might be in order to take revenge—which in turn might lead to counterrevenge and so on.

Fear, shame, and paranoia ran rampant. People would even occasionally ostracize their own family members to rid themselves of the disease. Over the course of the early years of the AIDS epidemic, the flames of distrust and blame were further fanned by the racial tensions underlying the Apartheid policies. Rumors and conspiracy theories were quite common. Some black people thought white people were infecting them deliberately; some white people fought desegregation because they believed it would spread AIDS into their communities. Some thought that AIDS was intentionally designed in laboratories, others claimed there was no connection between the HIV virus and AIDS. It was a mess. Our communities were clearly not prepared for what was happening.

The initial government response was to do nothing. They weren't willing to lift a finger. I talked to the

Department of Health again and again, only to be told that outreach campaigns were cost-prohibitive and not worth the effort. But I knew we had to do something: mobilize the community, organize gatherings, talk to the people working on the farms, and reach out to those who lived in remote areas. The true causes of AIDS, how vicious it was, and what could be done to prevent its spread needed to be told. I asked my boss from the Department of Health to let me use their vehicle at night for an awareness campaign I planned to organize. She wrote to Pretoria, and I was granted permission from them in writing. This letter of permission was a necessary document because I knew that the police would stop me at night to inquire about what I was doing, so I needed proof that I was on government business.

In the evenings I talked to any group that would listen; I distributed pamphlets and approached schools. I called the farms to try to get the farmers' support for organizing large gatherings of workers, telling the farmers a sick workforce would hit them economically. I spoke to the congregations of local churches, calling on our moral duty to help each other. Since I officiated at funerals as a lay minister, I would even speak up there, asking parents to protect their children. (This was against Zulu tradition, but I felt I had no other choice—I simply had to get through to people.)

In addition to large groups, I found myself preaching to most every person I met. I told unmarried people that sexual abstinence was best, but if that was not possible then the men should at least wear condoms. I urged those who had already contracted the disease to use contraception, so that they wouldn't give birth to children with AIDS. Over and over, I said, "There is no cure for this disease yet. We pray, we hope, but for now, there is not much we can do. Please watch out, please be careful. Please protect the health of your wife and your children."

So many of us were dying. Sometimes I felt death was everywhere I walked. Though I tried to stay with my patients through the worst of it, there were so many. To help with communication, I left old cell phones in homes where the parents were very sick. When they took a turn for the worse, their children would call me and I'd come over to help. Poor children! How scary it must have been for them to watch their parents die.

I met Promise, whom I later adopted, during this time. His father had already passed away, and now his mother was dying from AIDS. I was attending to her, and when I heard her breath changing and felt that the end was near, I asked her what I could do for her, if she wanted me to hold her hands. "No, please get my son Promise, I want Promise to hold my hands when I go." So I got Promise, who at the time was only nine years old. He stood by her bed, quietly, and took her hands. They looked at each other without speaking, and then she passed. He didn't cry and he didn't scream; I think he wanted to be brave for his mom. Only weeks later did he allow himself to cry.

More often than not, there was little I could do at the homes of the dying. I would sit with them to try to soothe their pain. Sometimes I would hold their hands; sometimes we'd just talk. Some wanted me to sing for them, so I'd sing them a Zulu song or a song from church. Some wanted us to pray together, yet others wanted to be quiet. When the end was near, I would always ask, "Do you want your children to see you die, or should I bring them outside?" And if they didn't want their children present, I would ask them if they wanted their children to see them after they'd gone. It was so painful!

You never get used to death. I don't know how many people I have seen dying, how many hands I've held, or how many times I have heard the last gasping sounds of those nearing their end. Too many. People say death is part of the natural cycle, and of course they are right. But each time I step outside the home of someone who has just died, my heart is heavy.

With AIDS, the flood of new patients overburdened the medical system. Mobile services couldn't do outreach, and I was quickly realizing I couldn't do the work by myself. So in 1989, with the help of several churches, we founded UHAI, the Underberg/Himeville AIDS Initiative. UHAI was set up primarily to coordinate outreach activities, but soon we expanded its range of tasks. We opened a little office in Himeville where people could come and get tested. If they tested positive, we would provide them with counseling and offer psychological, medical, and legal assistance.

We would help fill out paperwork, check on patients' families, and write hospital referrals—whatever was required.

In addition to the patients' needs, there were those of the families. The financial stress often meant school costs were prohibitive, so I helped families apply for government grants and approached school principals about dropping the uniform requirements. For basic necessities like food, I networked with CINDI (the Children in Distress Network) to receive assistance.

The government provided some aid, but they couldn't do everything, so the churches helped a lot too. In fact, the board of UHAI consisted entirely of church members. We needed all the help we could get, particularly when it came to distributing food to children, usually orphans. At one time I was feeding more than 80 children in Underberg and more than 120 in Himeville. I virtually didn't sleep anymore.

Many of the orphans lived in a kind of foster system with relatives, often their grandmothers, and there wasn't any centralized oversight. So after work I would drive around, making sure that each child had received his or her food parcel. If there was a problem I couldn't resolve right away, I would come back early the next morning. On Saturdays, I'd drive around to talk to the grannies and aunts who were looking after the orphans to make sure they could provide the children everything they needed. If they were lacking skills, I would organize training for them. It was a lot of work.

Back in '89, there were only two social workers for the entire area. If I directed them to a specific case, more often than not I would hear excuses, something like, "Oh, we are sorry, but the government vehicle broke down. There is no way for us to get there." So I would get into the car myself, pick up the children, and bring them to the center. I trained many community care workers, but there was no money for a salary or even a small stipend, so I lost most of them after a short time.

By 2000, I decided to retire from my job as a nurse at the community health center and focus full-time on our drop-in center, the outreach work, and the child-care for the families affected by AIDS.

Meanwhile, my oldest son Bheki had contracted HIV, and then soon after him his wife and their children. It was so painful to watch their demise! It seemed that Bheki had developed full-blown AIDS more quickly than people usually did, and he knew there was no cure. But I am very proud of him for what he did in the face of his prognosis. Rather than hiding in shame or resorting to revenge or hatred, he came clean about it and joined the outreach effort. When I went to talk to a group, he would often come with me, telling them, "Look at me! I am dying because I didn't listen, because I didn't want to know. For me, it is too late, but you still have a chance. Don't repeat my mistake. Protect yourself and your loved ones." It was heartbreaking to see him revealing his HIV status like this, but I think it had a huge impact, and I would like to believe that his courage saved many people's lives.

Though I felt all of my work during this time was necessary and rewarding, particularly close to my heart was my outreach to the orphans. Through my work with UHAI, I became sharply aware of just how many children were losing their parents, often when they were still toddlers. The community tried to absorb these children as best as it could, but families can only take so many. I remember a grandmother who was living with eighteen children. Sometimes when one mother would take in a late relative's children she would soon after become infected herself, leaving the children orphaned for a second time. So it wasn't that people were unwilling to help, but the crisis had reached a dimension that simply crushed any system in place.

Often, nobody even knew about an orphaned child. I remember once finding a scared girl sitting next to the corpse of her mother, who had passed away more than a week prior. She said she thought that her mother was sleeping and was afraid to leave her. Other times there was simply no place for a child to go. Little children, lost and forlorn, wandered the streets in search of something to eat.

Frequently, these children became infected with HIV as well. You see, when their parents were discharged from the hospital and sent home to die, who took care of them? Their children. The mothers often suffered from diarrhea, and the children, before going to school in the morning, would put diapers on their moms. Back then, nobody had disposable ones, so the children would wash the diapers by hand. The problem was that children frequently have little cuts and wounds on their hands, and when they washed the diapers, they got infected. To try to alleviate the problem, I called a hotel in the area and said, "Please give me your old towels you are no longer using. We need them badly." The people from the hotel were indeed kind enough to bring me a whole truckload. (Of course, storage was challenging. I had to buy plastic boxes in which I could store them outside.) Those proved to be very helpful. I would pick up the used diapers, disinfect them, and then the local laundry service was kind enough to launder them for free so they could be reused.

I also started building a new organization with volunteer caregivers who would go into patients' homes to help with the most basic needs and hygiene. Luckily, this time I already had some experience from my work in northern Zululand. I looked for volunteer workers among my church community and tried to pick those whose homes were in strategically located places. I used the curriculum I had developed in previous years and set up training sessions in a conference room in the local community care center. I also encouraged the community care workers (CCWs) to work closely together with the traditional healers; for one, I thought it would be good if they could learn from them, and I also wanted to make sure that the healers didn't feel excluded.

Each volunteer was responsible for taking care of the families surrounding their home. I would first go into the homes to ask permission to introduce a helper, and then I'd come back with CCWs. The CCWs would regularly check on their patients, alert them to the need of getting immunized against tetanus, provide basic medications, and even distribute food parcels to them.

The model worked so well that after only a year, we had an organization with about forty CCWs strategically placed throughout the communities. Of course, I couldn't pay anything, but in order to compensate them at least a little bit, I would make sure they had access to donated clothing and the food parcels. It wasn't much, but they were happy to help and could use the little we had to offer.

Whenever the CCWs didn't know what to do with a patient, they would call me, and I would either refer them to the hospital or provide basic hospice services. Many a night I visited homes and sat with the dying.

I did not pity the dead. I always told my children, "Those who've died are no longer in pain, they are on the other side, and one day we'll all meet over there." I pitied those who were left behind though—the mothers and fathers whose child had just passed, the boys and girls who had just lost a brother, a sister, or a friend. And above all I worried for the children who had just lost a mother or father, who were scared and didn't understand. Even if a child's mother was poor and sick, she was his mother, the one person he had relied on all his life. Children love their mothers, and when they find themselves without them, alone in the world, they are terrified. It's heartbreaking.

I remember burying one young lady who had worked on a farm. She left behind a two-year-old and a five-year-old. The woman had no relatives, and her husband had died before the second child was born. Even finding men who could help with the grave was challenging because it was the middle of the week and everybody was working on farms. So we buried the woman at 4:00 a.m., before the workday started. There we were, her two children sitting on my lap, tired and upset, watching as her coffin was lowered into the grave. They clutched me with their little hands, holding me as close as they could. I asked myself, "Are they scared because they see their mother going under the ground, or are they scared because they are afraid that I too might leave them?" It is those children that I worry for the most.

In the face of this orphan crisis, I found myself in a position I never thought I'd be in again. I had four children of my own who had lived with my sister back in Harding while I'd worked in Underberg. By then, all of them had left to start families of their own or to go study at the University of Durban. I thought I was done being a mother to young children. Plus, I was already over fifty. But when I saw these children, I knew I couldn't ignore my heart's call. So I started adopting again.

The first three children I took in were Princess, Angel, and Constance. The names of Zulu children often demonstrate the joy, love and hope their parents have for them. They lived on the farm where their parents had been employed. The dad had died two years before, when the mother was pregnant with the youngest. Now the mother too had succumbed to AIDS. After her death, I took the body, paid for and conducted the funeral, and the next day, went back to check on the children and to make sure they had enough food in the house. When I came and looked around, I realized they had nothing, not a crumb of anything. I talked to the farmer, who said it broke his heart to see the children of his workers suffering like this, but there was just no way he could take them in. I searched for relatives, but nobody seemed to know of any. There was one older sister, Ntethelelo, who had decided to stay on the farm to work, but she couldn't support the four of them. What could I do? The children were too young to fend for themselves and were open to all kinds of abuse. I just couldn't walk away. So after a break of more than twenty years, I became the mother of three small children.

I moved them into my place and found a lovely, kind nanny who could take care of them while I was at work during the day. Though I was still living in that small two-bedroom house, I enjoyed having the children there. I found a school for the older ones and a preschool for the smallest so she had playmates.

From then on, I adopted more children as I saw the need.

The next child was at an orphanage where I'd been bringing clothes that I'd collected in Underberg. She was—like my first child—of black and Indian heritage; her name was Gugu, which means "precious."

Nobody seemed to take care of the little one because she was mixed (people were often still quite prejudiced at that time), so I took her in.

Then there was Ntombi. When she was a newborn, her mother had put her in a plastic bag and dumped her into a garbage bin somewhere in Durban; her umbilical cord was still attached when a garbage worker found her by chance. I was thinking of her mother when I gave the little one her name: Ntombi means "let us forgive." When she came to me, she was only a few months old and she suffered from severe asthma and all sorts of allergies. The social worker begged me to take her because there was no one else who could have cared for her properly.

Then another baby was dropped outside on my doorstep. I heard a baby's cries, and when I went outside, I found a cute little girl. When I looked into her face, I thought I knew who her mother might be, so I went to the police and asked them to search for the mother. Sure enough, the woman was found, but she was sick as could be, and what was worse, she was confused; the AIDS virus had already affected her brain. Probably somebody had feared for the child's safety and taken her to my doorstep to protect her. So I eventually adopted this one too.

More and more children came, and within just a few years, I had twelve of them living with me.

My place had been small to begin with. It was a two-bedroom house with one bedroom being used as the residential clinic. This meant I shared the other bedroom and the kitchen with twelve children. Let's just say it now seemed really small. First I raised my bed onto cinder blocks, so that some could sleep on top and some underneath. A second bed on the other side of the room was also raised and the space underneath it used for storage. Those who didn't fit on the beds would sleep in the small space between the bedroom and the kitchen or on the kitchen floor. At night, a child's body covered practically every spot, so you didn't know where to step.

Of course, this situation wasn't tenable, and I knew in the long run we needed a larger place, but for the time being it was quite nice. I liked having all my children close by; it was very harmonious, even cozy. And most rewarding was seeing the children brighten up and become happier by the month.

Fortunately food wasn't a problem, as we got a lot of support from the community around us. Farmers would give me some milk or potatoes, and the churches would put together food parcels. And then we had our gardens! I've always loved gardening. Even as a child, it gave me great joy to plant things and see them grow. When Ms. McKechnie gave me seeds for, say, carrots, I would be so proud when I could bring her some of the carrots I had grown myself. Of course, my early gardening was also motivated by a very basic drive: hunger. If I wanted to have something to eat throughout the year, I had better plan my gardening very carefully. Over the years, I learned how to build a winter garden, how to scare away animals who would try to eat my vegetables (Chomi was a great help!), and when best to harvest. Later, as an adult, I met Mr. Maszibukho, a true gardening genius who introduced me to organic gardening. Of course, back then we thought the best thing about "organic" was that it was cheap, as we didn't have to buy pesticides or synthetic fertilizers. Only later did I learn to appreciate the health aspects of organic food. Mr. Maszibukho showed me how to apply fertilizer in trenches, how to grow fruits and vegetables without using too much water, and a million other things. But regardless of the methods, I simply love gardening, and it was such a basic and deep joy to serve my children what our gardens produced.

To motivate the children to help, each child got his or her own little patch and could determine what they wanted to grow on "their" patch. Oh, how proud they were when we could harvest their produce! They also shared responsibility. When one child wasn't done with homework and couldn't go out to tend to her patch, another child would take over. We grew carrots and cabbage, spinach and peppers, cauliflower, broccoli, onions. We always had such healthy food from our garden.

In spite of the challenges, it was a happy time.

The rondavel where Abegail grew up.

Mancini, Abegail's mother.

Paternal aunt Adelaide.

Paternal aunt Matha, who died at 104.

Abegail's graduation from the University of Natal, 1989.

Family of Reverend Johanson, who helped Abegail find holiday
jobs to fund her purchase of clothing and other necessities.

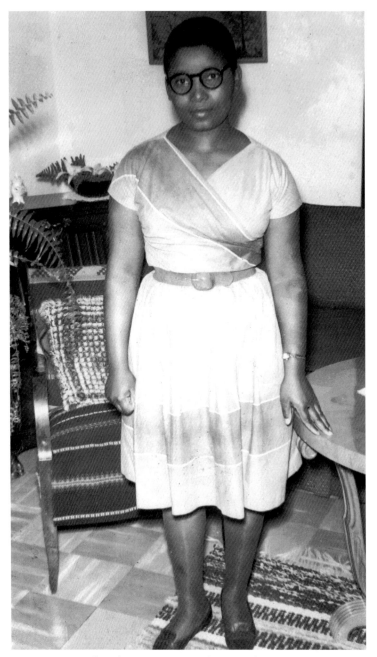

Abegail at age twenty, working as a domestic
servant in Port Shepstone.

Sister Abegail
(center)
with Sisters
Jane Ngcobo
and
Khle Dlamini,
1966.

Sister Abegail (far right) at Elim Hospital in northern Polokwane.

Abegail's graduation from the University of Natal.

Abegail, age thirty-six, at nursing school graduation.

Abe at thirty-two (right) with friend Doris Bekwa.

Abegail with first group of adopted orphans.

Happy moments with children at Clouds.

One big family.

On the jungle gym donated by community members.

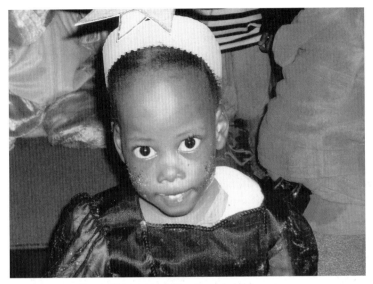

One of Sister Abegail's adopted children, 2009.

Sister and brother, 2009.

Training community care workers.

Abegail on the way to a lecture about AIDS, 2005.

Abegail with a plaque in her honor at the youth center in Mqatsheni.

Abegail receives an Exploration Award, which was given to nurses
for outstanding community service and outreach, 1979.

At Clouds, 2009.

In London, dancing the "Shosholoza," 2009.

Sister Abegail receives the Unsung Heroes of Compassion
Award from the Dalai Lama in 2009.

5

Hope and Rising Up

As the pandemic spread, yet another alarming facet of the orphan crisis became increasingly prevalent: the abuse of girls and young women. It began when a growing number of families in the area were headed up by children, often no older than twelve or thirteen. When their parents died, these brave girls would be responsible for getting food and other necessities for their younger siblings. Though the community helped, these girls were mainly dependent on government support, most often from the Department of Social Welfare— and this system was failing.

Corruption had infested nearly every layer of bureaucracy and power. To prove the loss of a parent, you needed a death certificate, but most people didn't even have a birth certificate, let alone a death certificate. Then some churches, like the Bantu Presbyterian Church, had a lot of nonsensical rules concerning Western medicine. They didn't allow their members to see a doctor or to take medicine, nor did they allow the use of a mortuary for the deceased; so who was to certify a death? Without proof of a parent's death, you couldn't apply for support for the children. It was so frustrating! Then, even if all of the hindrances were somehow removed, pretty much every level of power, from the top bureaucrats to the local offices down to the individual policemen, all claimed a share of the aid money. Without getting their shares, they would block the money's distribution. The children were at the very bottom of that stream, and often what trickled down to them was barely enough for their survival.

It was truly shameful to witness how people in power took advantage of those who had no protection at all. Increasingly horrible stories surfaced. I heard of a boy who starved to death outside the compound of the heavily guarded social welfare office that distributed money to those in need. The little boy had money waiting for him inside, but he couldn't afford the bribes requested by the guards to give him access to the office.

With so much confusion and lack of oversight in the system, it's no surprise that sexual deviants began preying on young girls. These poor girls bore the full weight of responsibility for their little siblings, yet they had no one to look out for them. Without parents, and in a community overwhelmed by the pandemic and hindered by a defunct police system, they were completely open to molestation. I knew one girl who received her welfare through a policeman. Each time he would deliver the money, she had to first drive with him into a forest. She was only thirteen. What could this poor thirteen-year-old do? Had she refused the policeman, she would have put the lives of her siblings at risk. It was a terrible burden to bear.

When I learned of this, I sued the policeman, determined to bring the man to justice. But soon I learned there is no justice in South African justice. The case was simply transferred to another district and then another district and then another district—until it disappeared into some drawer. The other policemen, the man's superiors, and the judges—they all covered for him.

Of course, there were people with a sense of decency, people who did what they could to help. Whenever there is great suffering, there are always those who heed its call. But they couldn't do enough to prevent all of the damage. Through my work for UHAI, I was acutely aware of the situation, but with twelve children already living with me, my hands were bound; I just couldn't take more in. So I tried to raise awareness about the issue and help the children in question as best I could, even when I felt it was an uphill battle.

This was when the miracle occurred—the miracle of compassion.

It began when an American named Roger Teeter was traveling in the area on vacation and happened to hear about me. He took an interest in our situation and came to visit. He said, "So, who are these children?" and I told him, "These are my orphan children." "Where do they sleep?" I showed him. He asked many questions, and then he looked at me kindly. "Sister Abe," he said, "I would like to help. What is it that you need the most? Do you need money to feed and clothe the children? How can I help?"

"Mr. Roger," I said, "thank you. It is very generous of you to ask, but we don't need money; we have enough food and clothes. We get food parcels from the community, and generous people like you often donate their hand-me-down clothes. So we are fine. But you see, there are many households here that are headed by children because AIDS has taken their parents. These children are subject to the most terrible abuse, and I would love to help them, but there is simply no more space in my home. What we really need is a bigger home so I can take these children in and protect them."

He looked at me and said, "OK, let me go home to Seattle and talk to the members of my church. Let's see what we can do."

He left, and month after month I waited. My children asked, "Is this American man going to help us find a bigger house?" And I told them, "You must pray that he won't rest until he has found the means to help. You must pray to God." It was very funny when I heard them in their evening prayers saying, "Dear Father, we pray that this American not sleep at night until he has found us a bigger house."

Then one day, about half a year later, a man came to the drop-in center where I was working. I seemed to recall his face but didn't know his name. "Do you remember me?" he said. "I'm Roger." I was so happy to see him. I gave him a hug, and tears streamed down my face. "I have got something for you," he said. "Can you come with me? I need to show you something."

He led me to a farmhouse that had belonged to one of the doctors at our hospital. I knew the house well. At one point the doctor had fallen sick, and when his primary nurse had gone on vacation, I'd come to look after him there for a while. When the doctor had died, his son didn't want to live in Underberg and had sold the house and the land surrounding it. As it turned out, the buyer was a charity Roger had started on our behalf! I couldn't believe it! I remember the day as if it were yesterday—it was the first of July. All night long I cried and cried from happiness. When I got up in the morning, it started snowing. It felt like we were being blessed by God!

I never learned the price of the farm. Roger just told me it was his form of personal tithing and that his church had helped. They also bought us our first vehicle, a bus for sixteen people, and a little later a car that could seat eight. They were so very generous!

As soon as we moved into our new home, I could fulfill my wish and adopt the children who were vulnerable to abuse. In just one month, the number of orphans I cared for jumped from twelve to forty-seven. To help raise them, we paid a little stipend to three women from the community. Since this was a job that required both experience and a twenty-four-hour-a-day commitment, I chose single women whose own children had already left home.

When we moved in, Roger asked me what we should name the place. His suggestion was "Abegail's Nest." This was a very nice name, but I didn't like the idea of its being tied to a person. It was God who had given us that place. I thought about it, and came back with something different: "How about 'Clouds of Hope'?" Clouds are good things in South Africa, because we often need rain. Also, just as rain pours from clouds, so do we want our message of hope to pour from our place. "What do you think?" I asked. "It's a fine name," Roger said, and the board approved it.

By 2001, there were fifty-one people living at Clouds of Hope. We planted gardens around the house, purchased some animals—mainly chickens and cows—and created a little pond. We also cleared some land so that the children could run around and play soccer. It was a really nice setup. In the evenings, we'd sit together, and if there was time, I'd teach the children songs while I played the guitar.

During the first two years, until 2003, I continued to run the UHAI drop-in center. Its chief aim was to test people for HIV, and if they tested positive, to get them to the hospital for treatment. Since there were still so many patients, I had to do this trip every month, which was very time-consuming. With my involvement in the outreach work and nearly fifty children at home, I couldn't keep up with everything, so I gave up that responsibility in 2003.

Of course, with so many people living under one roof, none of us had any more space than when I'd had twelve children in my little house, but I didn't worry about that. Instead I wondered how we could accommodate the many more children out there who had lost parents and were in dire need of help.

As a solution, we applied for government grants to build cottages on the property so we could house more children. South African bureaucracy is slow and cumbersome, but fortunately we had the advantage of being a known and proven entity. After all, UHAI had successfully received many grants and all the board members of UHAI were now board members of Clouds. Our case had a better chance than most, but even with that advantage, I knew it would take years.

Then one day, I overheard a conversation that lent more urgency to our expansion plans. A social worker from the Department of Social Welfare visited Clouds to check on the children and make sure they were well taken care of. I heard him ask one of the children, "Do you love your mom?" The child looked at him, confused, and asked, "Which one?" After all, there were the three women and myself, so the child didn't know who her mother was. After thinking about it, I decided that needed to be changed. A child should have one person as a point of reference; every child should have one mother.

If the proposed cottages were built, then we could have six children live in each cottage with one mother. This, I thought, would give them a clear sense of belonging and of home.

When Roger came the next year and asked what he could do for us, I told him that the government had approved our grant application but that it could take years for them to actually transfer the money. I said, "We have forty-seven children living in one house, with another child on the way. We need to build these cottages." Roger once again agreed to help us, this time with a bridging fund. He lent us the money for the cottages with the understanding that once we received the government grants, we'd pay him back. We started work on the cottages immediately. Within just three years, we had built twelve cottages, each serving as the home for six children and one mother.

I was so happy to have houses for the children! Of course, with so many of them it was a very busy time, but it was worth every minute. I still lived in the main house with the eighteen children whom I had legally adopted and given my name. My day started around 4:00 a.m. I'd first cook the porridge for breakfast, then set aside the different medications for those who needed them and prepare everything else for the day. Then I'd wake up the children and check on them. Those who were sick stayed in bed, while the others got up to bathe and get ready for school. They developed their own system, but whenever one was done, she came to me and said, "Gogo, I am ready," and then the next one went in.

After baths, we'd have breakfast. Of course, it was crowded, so some sat on the floor, some on mats, some on the sofa. They all wanted me to sit with them, so I had to rotate the whole time. Maybe it would've been easier if we'd eaten in shifts, but I've always felt a family should share meals. It's such a lovely and important time to be together.

Then I would drive the kids to their different schools, and afterward go home to pick up the ill ones and take them to the hospital. On the way, we usually collected donations; for example, Mr. Knox from our local supermarket was kind enough to donate day-old bread rolls to all of Clouds. Once home, I would begin the washing and laundering, scrubbing and cleaning. If there was time left before leaving to pick the kids up, I would go out to the vegetable garden to water plants and see which ones needed care and which ones could be harvested. Oh, how I love my gardens! Seeing all the plants and fruits and vegetables grow is one of my delights, and they provide such delicious and nourishing organic food.

After picking up the children from school, I'd check notes from the teachers and talk to the kids about what had happened during the day. Then I needed to make sure they did their homework, which usually took several hours. For grades one and two I would check all of the homework myself, but the older children helped supervise each other. Whenever one of them had a question, he or she would come to me and I'd try to help.

If one of them got into trouble at school, I would sit her down. "Darling," I would ask, "what happened to you that you did that? What made you act that way? I know it's not you, so why did you do it?" For the most part, talking about it would clear the air.

After homework, supper needed to be prepared, and we'd all come together again to eat. Then, if there were any time left in the day, we'd sit and play games or sing until bedtime. I read the little ones a story and talked some more to the older ones, trying to make certain I didn't overlook any of their worries from the day. They all had their own personalities and their own ways, so I had to be very careful to pay enough attention to each.

As in any family, some children needed more care than others, but I would like to think we all tried to ensure that each of us got what was necessary. It isn't right to reject a child because he or she has more difficulties than another. Everyone deserves love and someone to watch out for him or her. I remember a couple of years ago I got a call from a social worker who told me he had a baby he needed to bring over. "The little girl needs a home," he explained. I asked what had happened. "Well," he said, "Busisiwe's mother was only fourteen years old when she gave birth to her. The father is unknown. Tragically, the mother had full-blown AIDS, which she has passed on to Busisiwe."

I was speechless, a mother with full-blown AIDS at fourteen? She must have been raped and infected at a very young age. "Now, the mother died just three days after delivering the baby," he continued, "and to make matters worse, the girl is not only HIV positive but is said to be blind, deaf, and mentally retarded. Oh yes, and she has a heart problem. She will not live longer than a year." Oh my, I thought, what a terrible start in life! Poor thing! No wonder the hospital didn't have the resources to take care of her. As I learned later, the only known relative of the child, a grandmother, had told the hospital not to bother informing her when the child died. It was a shame; nobody wanted the poor little thing! "Can you please take her, Sister Abe?" the social worker pleaded.

What a sad sight Busisiwe was in the beginning. She had a huge head and a body that was floppy, as if without any muscles. She was completely paralyzed, and so her head was drooping. Her eyes were empty, sores covered her body, and her breath rattled and wheezed. I asked the other mothers, "Please, we need to find a spot for her." But they said, "Sister, we would like to help, but with all her open sores and her being positive, there is no way. We are sorry."

So I took her in. The first time I tried feeding her she choked. When I looked closely I noticed that the hospital had been feeding her through a nasal tube. It was not easy; she required so much care. I made her sleep in my bed so I could spend as much time as possible with her. Little by little she improved, and slowly she began to take in food. As much as I could, I held her in my arms and talked to her, but the first few months, I got no response from her. Then, one happy day, I noticed her trying to lift her hand! I was so excited! She is not paralyzed, I thought, and I immediately started doing exercises with her. Then another day I noticed when I entered the room, she was trying to turn toward me. So she wasn't deaf either! She had been completely misdiagnosed. Lo and behold, Busisiwe slowly came around, and three years later she has turned out to be a beautiful young child who can speak and sing and who goes to preschool. Her heart appears to be healing and she is taking to the antiviral drugs very well. She still can't walk, but I know it's just a matter of time, because she is already trying to crawl. We are so proud of her; Busisiwe is a miracle, a true inspiration for all of us.

Many of the children who came to us had suffered greatly. They had been through the death of their parents, abject poverty, and all kinds of abuse, including sexual. It is understandable that some of them experienced psychological problems: grief, depression, anger, fear of abandonment, and lack of trust are just a few. Fortunately, as a psychiatric nurse I have experience in this area, and so whenever I saw a child who needed special attention, I designed a development program for him or her and also requested the supervision of a child psychologist with whom I could discuss my program. Sometimes a very small change made a big difference. For instance, if a child is angry and aggressive, a lot of physical activity may be good. If a child is shy and insecure, extra responsibility can improve self-confidence. I went on a short walk with each of these children every day during which they talked to me about what troubled them.

To track the development of the children, I kept a little log of their behavior. In some cases, we noticed that something was a bit off, even if it didn't manifest itself as a behavioral issue. Take the case of Nanny, a four-year-old girl. She behaved quite normally and got along well with the other children. But after a while I noticed she would go several times a day to the gate and just stand there and look out for a while. Then she'd return. So one day I went over to her. "Nanny, why are you always standing at the gate?" "Gogo," she said, "when my father was buried, they told me he would never come back. But when my mother was buried, I was crying and crying, and they told me that one day she would come back and she would bring me nice clothes and sweets, and we would live together again. So I stopped crying. And now, I am afraid she doesn't know that I am here at Clouds, so I go to the gate to make sure she sees me." "Oh Nanny," I said, "we need to talk." And I sat with her and we spoke about death. I read to her from a book I use in a bereavement course for children and then I told her, "Nanny, let's take some clay and mold your mother's body and then we'll have the boys build a coffin and we will bury her." We did that, and after a little ceremony, we talked some more. "You see, Nanny, now when you think of your mother, don't go to the driveway, because she won't come. Instead, go to her grave and put down a rose for her. She would have liked that." For the next two weeks, that's what Nanny did every day. The third week, she came to me. "Gogo, I know my mom will never come back. I don't want to go to the grave anymore." And that was that.

Though many of the children had difficulties to overcome, there was always joy. Some weekdays, but particularly on the weekend, the children went outside to play soccer or netball or just run around. I joined in the soccer game as much as I could, but of course in my mid-seventies, it wasn't easy to keep up with them! But if I was tired, I would be the referee, and if I was too exhausted for even that, I would play the spectator. Children have such a desire to be seen and acknowledged; it was good for them if I watched. As a spectator, it was my job to come up with names for them; say, if a child was particularly small, I would cheer for the "short division," or something else funny. Children love that kind of thing!

After the game, I'd often take out a tub of ice cream. First, I might tease them: "Oh, I worked so hard, I think I deserve ice cream." Of course, they all came running. "Gogo, Gogo, we worked very hard too! We think we deserve ice cream too." Then we'd all sit together and enjoy the treat. Those were happy moments.

Caring for the children, running the orphanage, doing outreach work in the community, and fulfilling my duties as a lay minister—these things could easily take a toll on me. After all, every day new problems required attention, frustrations and disappointments occurred, and suffering had to be addressed. It was sometimes overwhelming, and when we are overwhelmed, we risk closing our hearts and losing ourselves. Because of that, I began a practice (that I have since continued) that helps me to let go, cleanse myself, and stay grounded.

When I was a child, I loved to perform Zulu dances at weddings and other celebrations. It was a natural way of releasing tension. Zulu dances are very physical, involving a lot of stomping, jumping, and shouting, and I remember always feeling calm and clean afterward; somehow, being fully in your body helps clear your mind. Of course, at my age jumping and stomping like a wild animal would probably not be so wise. Instead I have found another way to help me deal with frustrations and worries.

Every night I get up at 3:00 a.m. With so many children, there is always one that is sick and one that can't sleep or has nightmares—but by 3:00 a.m. the house has usually quieted down. So, I get up and if everything is calm, I sit somewhere by myself and let the previous day pass by. I reflect on everything that happened that day; one incident after another, big or small, good or bad, and I let everything pass through my mind. It's a bit like what I learned as a teenager in Christian camp. I acknowledge what happened and how it affected me, and then I let it go; whether happy or sad, I let it all go. Then, when I feel clean of tension and pure of heart, I start praying. I pray for my children; I pray for my family; I pray for my friends; and I pray for all people who are suffering. I pray for their health and well-being, that they may be free from suffering and that they may find joy and peace in their lives. This prayer makes me feel very good. Sometimes, by the time I have finished, the first child is already waking up and I go start to prepare breakfast, and sometimes, if everyone is still asleep, I go back to bed for another hour. It's a nightly ritual I have come to really appreciate.

You see, I think we all need some kind of release. I like my children to play soccer. Running and chasing after a ball is very healthy for them, not just physically but also emotionally. Of course, what's right differs from person to person and from one phase in our life to another. It may be chasing a ball, stomping on the ground, or praying. Sometimes we may need all three. Whatever works best, it is important to take good care of ourselves, so we can give our all to those who need and deserve it most.

I knew there were more communities that needed help beyond the area surrounding Clouds of Hope, and I was continually thinking about what more I could do for them. Among the many poor areas, one had always stood out, a place high up in the Drakensberg Mountains, right along the border to Lesotho, called Mqatsheni. I had fallen in love with this area over twenty years before, when I first ventured there in my fight against leprosy and TB. The mountains are spectacularly beautiful, the valleys wide and majestic. Getting there, however, was very difficult—so difficult, in fact, that Mrs. Strydom hadn't wanted me to try because she thought it would ruin our car. Even today, there is only one dirt road that leads up there.

Because of Mqatsheni's high elevation, the air is pretty thin and the slopes of the mountains are prone to vicious hail and thunderstorms. People live far apart, often not even in shouting distance from each other. Most of the families living there own a patch of land they try to cultivate with maize and potatoes and a couple of fruit trees. It's very difficult to eke out a living as there is obviously no employment there. If your patch of land gets destroyed by hail, you are hard-pressed to find anything to eat for a long time. For water, people rely on the rain, and sometimes weeks or even months go by without a drop. There is no electricity, no medical services, no stores, nothing.

I remember when I first went to Mqatsheni. I set up my mobile station, and word soon got out. People came from all over the mountains to see me. I'm sure some of them had never had medical help. Many of them died on the way because they were too weak for the trip or because their horse lost its footing on the treacherous mountain paths.

The area is prone to accidents, and its people often had to resort to the most primitive methods to help themselves. When a child would break an arm or a leg, an adult usually simply stepped on the fracture to straighten it out, and then they would bind two pieces of wood around it to keep it in place. I once saw a child who had been treated this way, and I asked the man who brought him in how the child had coped with the pain. "Oh, you see, Sister," he said, "they usually pass out from pain, but they always wake up at some point."

But what the area lacked in resources, it made up for in natural beauty and in the kindness of its people.

Nobody had any money to pay for medical services, so instead people would show their gratitude by bringing me fruit from their land. I remember them offering peaches—big, juicy yellow peaches, the most delicious I had ever tasted. They were also supportive of each other as a community. If a child needed medical attention and the parents were too sick to transport the child, inevitably somebody else from the community would make the journey. Neighbors would build stretchers and carry those who couldn't walk. Help was provided with the same grace with which the peaches were offered. It was really a very loving community.

Over the years, I had been successful in eradicating leprosy in the area, but when the AIDS pandemic hit, we were virtually back to square one. The people were uneducated and completely unprepared, so the disease just ravaged the area. There was no medicine, no hospital, no hope.

I remember when a child from the area was brought to the clinic in Underberg. I asked him where his mother was. "She died," the boy said. "And your father?" The same. "And your grandparents?" The same. "Where do you and your siblings live then, and who takes care of you?" One of the ladies with whom the child had come said, "They live with a very, very old woman who can't walk anymore. That's why I am here with the child." The name of that old lady was Mama Josie Mjwara, and she turned out to be the great-granny of the children.

So the following Saturday I drove up there. I had to take my own car because I was not allowed to use a government vehicle on the weekend. I asked somebody, "Can you please tell me where Mama Josie Mjwara lives? I have clothes and food for her." When I finally arrived at her little place, I found her lying on her bed. She was ninety-six years old and couldn't move anymore. Her teeth were completely filed down from whatever she had been chewing, and she was clearly in severe pain. Imagine, ninety-six years old and she still had to take care of these children! She had seen every single one of her own offspring die, and then every single one of her grandchildren. And now she was the only one left to take care of her great-grandchildren. When I gave her the food and the clothes, tears were running down her cheeks, she was so happy.

This was an area clearly in great need, and when the AIDS crisis hit, the people were devastated. At the time, with my Clouds work and so many children to take care of, I knew I'd have to leave the bulk of the work to others. Within the next few years, I helped train some community care workers, drawing on my experience back when I worked in northern Zululand and in the Underberg area. I trained local women in palliative care, AIDS testing and counseling, the administration of simple medicines, and everything else that was needed to provide basic support to families who had no access to other resources. These women go from home to home, checking on patients, providing medicine, and setting up liaisons with the hospital or social workers. I was happy to help, in a small way, to develop resources for Mqatsheni and bring support to an area that is close to my heart.

6

Rewards

In 2006, Jenny Rogers, a friend from Durban who would later work as a volunteer fundraiser for Clouds, came to visit me. "Abe," she said, "I saw an article in the news last week that talked about a 'Woman of the Year' award, and I have submitted your name. What do you think?" Well, this didn't mean much to me, as I didn't even know what this prize was and who awarded it. "It's donated by Shoprite and SABC," she said. Shoprite is the largest South African retail chain, and SABC stands for South African Broadcasting Corporation. "Oh, OK," I said. "That will be fine, I guess." I think I forgot about the whole thing even before our conversation was over.

Four or five months later, I received a call from a man who said I had been selected as a finalist for the award and asked whether they could come with a camera team and shadow me for a few days. "Yes," I said, "that will be fine." So they sent a team of four over to Clouds.

I remember the first day of their stay happened to be the day when I drove up to Mqatsheni to deliver food parcels. Right as we were climbing up the old dirt road into the mountains, my pickup truck broke down. "Oh, please don't film that. It's a really good car," I told them. But they only laughed. They followed me all day, and by the time evening came around, they were very tired. But they really wanted to see what I was doing, so they stayed up with me as I told bedtime stories to the children—truthfully, I think they would have loved to go to sleep themselves.

A little later that night, I got a phone call. A woman was in very bad health, could I please come and assist? So I got ready and the poor camera team felt they had to come with me. The sick woman's place was only five kilometers from Clouds, but by the time we arrived it was clear we couldn't bring her back to health. She was dying. So I asked her how I could help her best. Would she like to talk? She shook her head. Would she like me to sing for her? No. Would she like me to hold her? She nodded yes. So we sat together and I held her in my arms until she passed away. Her teenage daughter was so shaken with shock and grief that I had to hold her too for many hours. Then the arrangements had to be made for the mortuary. By the time we left the house, a new day was already dawning. The team was very emotional from what they had just witnessed, and they were also exhausted. "When do you ever sleep?" they asked me. "Oh, I am very fortunate," I told them. "I don't need much sleep. You go and rest, and I'll see you later."

A few weeks after the team stayed with me, I was invited for two days to Jo'burg, where I was interviewed

about my life at Clouds and about my work in Under-
berg and with UHAI. At the end of my stay, I was told
I was now among the three finalists for my category,
Social Welfare. On August 7, I was flown to Cape
Town for an orientation session. The award ceremony
was set for the 8th, the Day of the Woman.

About eight hundred people gathered. A total of
thirty-six finalists were there, covering twelve different
categories. It was festive, with speeches and video clips
of all of the candidates. To add drama, the MC paused
each time before announcing the winner of a category.
When they came to Social Welfare, he seemed to pause
for a particularly long time. "And the winner is . . .
Sister Abegail Ntleko!" It was very fun.

I was happy for the award, because it came with a
little bit of money that I could distribute among my
children and the housemothers. My trophy was a glass
sculpture with an honorary inscription etched into it
(one of my children broke it later on). But the best
part was that all the children at Clouds could watch
the ceremony on TV. They were so excited to see me,
and afterward they called me in the hotel to tell me all
about it. Just to see their joy was my biggest award.

Two years later, in 2008, Jenny Rogers came to me
again. "I hope you don't mind," she said, "but I have
done something rather unusual. I have submitted your
name for a very special award. After all, it worked
out last time, no?" "What award is that?" I asked her.
"Well," she replied, "it's the Unsung Heroes of Compassion Award given by His Holiness the Dalai Lama."

Now, this time I have to admit I was speechless. The Dalai Lama, really? I had read some of his books and was very moved by his story. He seemed bigger than life, and I could not imagine ever meeting him in person. I really didn't believe it would happen; after all, many names would be submitted. I thought we would never even hear back from them.

But a few months later, Jenny came back. I could tell she was really excited. "You won't believe it," she said. "You have been selected by His Holiness. They are inviting us to America, to San Francisco, for you to receive the award!" Of course, I was excited about the opportunity to meet the Dalai Lama, but I was also worried. I had never been outside South Africa; how would I get a visa? Plus, I was seventy-five years old; could I survive such a long flight? And who would take care of the children while I was gone?

A few days later, however, I calmed down. After all, I had wanted to go to the American embassy in Durban anyway. I'd read about an American AIDS emergency fund and wanted to see whether some of that money could possibly be used for the training of community care workers. So the following week, I went to Durban and found myself successful on both counts: we would get some funding for training, and I would be issued a visa.

His Holiness's organization Wise Giving paid for our tickets to San Francisco, and Jenny took care of the travel arrangements. When the day came, I was still a bit nervous but also really happy. Jenny had family in

London, and she thought it would be a good idea to break up the long flight by staying a few days in England. Kittisaro and Thanissara, my Buddhist friends, had contacts in London who offered to host us. They were lovely gentlemen! But after a while, I noticed Jenny becoming more and more nervous. "Don't you see what's going on here?" she whispered to me. "Do you understand what's happening?" I had to smile. "Jenny, if you are talking about our hosts being gay, yes, thank you, I have noticed." "But you are a staunch Christian. Don't you care?" I looked at her and said, "Jenny, these lovely men have been kind enough to invite us into their home. From all I can see, they are wonderful people and I am not here to judge anybody. I am just grateful for their hospitality." After that, she seemed more relaxed, even relieved.

We were also very fortunate to find good accommodations in San Francisco. Our friend Eugene Cash (founding teacher of San Francisco Insight) and his wife, Pam, had visited us in South Africa, and now graciously invited us to stay with them. The Buddhist community of San Francisco welcomed us with open arms. Many of our meditation friends there went out of their way to introduce us to different groups and schools, drove us around, and made many connections between us and many groups.

Then the big day came.

The night before, Jenny and I stayed in the Ritz-Carlton. I had never been in a hotel like that, and I remember in the evening lying in bed and watching

TV on a screen that was nearly as big as the kitchen in my old place back home. The next morning was the ceremony. There were forty-nine honorees that year, and each one of them was introduced individually. There were monks and nuns, doctors and professors, householders and very simple people. Some six hundred guests had gathered to celebrate the honorees.

Jenny was so excited. She said if she could have one wish fulfilled it would be to touch His Holiness once in her life. But we were told to stay put when His Holiness came into the room, that getting up or bowing to him would create too much commotion. I prayed and told Jenny, "I'm sure your wish will come true." So there he came, a beautiful smile on his face, bowing humbly to all of us. He crossed the room, seeming to be looking straight at Jenny, and came to our table, and of the six hundred people in the room, Jenny was the only one for whom he stopped, for a moment clasping his hands around hers. Jenny burst out in tears. She couldn't believe it. Even in the following weeks, whenever she recalled this moment, she would tear up.

Jack Kornfield, a revered Buddhist teacher from California, gave a wonderful speech. Then the honorees were introduced. It was so moving and humbling to hear their stories. One had gone to war zones and helped children there, another had built up a food chain for homeless people, yet another had founded an organization that fought childhood leukemia. There were so many amazing stories, so many outstanding people. What an honor to be there!

His Holiness put a silken scarf around each honor-ee's neck (the scarf had frazzled loose threads, symbol-izing the impermanence of life), then took our hands in his, blessing each one of us. We were so touched. I think every single one of us cried as we descended from the stage. There is something about His Holiness's presence that shook us all to the core. The ceremony lasted seven or eight hours, followed by a delicious meal and a wonderful celebration.

That night, I could hardly sleep. I paced up and down, thinking about the day, looking at my scarf. I was so excited. Jenny said, "Abe, come to bed. Tomor-row is going to be a long day. The trip back is exhaust-ing, and you must rest." But I told her that this wasn't a night to sleep. It was a night to stay awake and feel the energy and the blessing we had been given.

7

Transitions

Around 2009, my standing at Clouds of Hope began to change. Due to my age, the board asked me to step down as the general manager. Biblically speaking, they argued, God gives us seventy years, and every year beyond that is just a gift. Since I had passed that mark, they felt it would not be responsible for me to stay at the helm.

Stepping down did unburden me of a lot of administrative tasks and allowed me to spend more time with my children, so for that I was happy. Over the course of the next few years, however, significant differences emerged between the new management and me. For example, I'd had every new child tested for HIV because I wanted to know what we were up against. The new manager, however, thought there was no need to do so unless a child became sick. His perspective unfortunately took precedence over mine.

The differences in our approaches showed even more when it came to psychological problems. Many of our children had been severely traumatized, so I felt this was an area that needed special attention. I have always believed that psychological problems need to be addressed before they develop into behavioral issues. But the management didn't feel the same about the need for psychological evaluation or treatment.

I remember the case of one young boy who was disturbed. From the beginning I lobbied for psychotherapy for him but couldn't get approval. Later it turned out that he'd started abusing other children in the orphanage. Such a shame. Fortunately, new management just recently took over. I hope they will be more receptive to implementing therapeutic support for the children.

It was difficult for me to stand by and watch things change in ways I disagreed with, but when I pointed to an issue, I wasn't respected. I was "just" an ordinary housemother and it was no longer my place to advise how to run the place. Sometimes I felt they were concerned I was threatening their authority. It was so sad! That was never my intention, and I was willing to follow their directives. So I did what I was told, but it was hard to keep quiet, particularly when I saw things that were disturbing and could do nothing about them.

Our relationship deteriorated further when I received the award from the Dalai Lama. Those who were very strongly Christian felt I shouldn't have accepted, that I had taken "prizes from the devil," while at the same time they requested that I hand over the "evil award money." It was really quite shameful!

In the end, the situation became untenable when there was pressure for me to move out of the main house where I lived with my adopted and fostered children. This would have split up my family. I was informed my children would be distributed across the cottages and I would no longer be required to work as a mother. Instead they designated me to become a fundraiser.

When I heard this, I didn't reply but just quietly went back to my room and sat down. I thought very hard for a long time. Clouds of Hope had been my dream; its children are my children. There was a whole community around Clouds, and so many people had helped with their generosity to make this dream come alive—could I really walk away from all this? Even more important, how could I leave behind the children who lived in the cottages? While I had not been their immediate mother, I felt very close to them. Whenever they had a problem with, say, their housemother, they would come to me. "Gogo, my mother is cross with me. What can I do?" And then we would talk it through. I was a buffer for them. All these children had already lost their parents; how would they feel if it seemed as if yet another person was abandoning them?

At the same time, it was clear to me that those influencing the decisions at the time preferred me out of their way and hence tried to cast me in a role I simply could not accept. My children were living together as a family; to separate them into different cottages meant in effect breaking up our entire family, and that, to me, was inconceivable. And there were other signs that were hard to ignore. Of course, I can't know for sure what the new leaders' exact intentions were, but many of my children started to feel discriminated against; when there were paper or pens, biscuits or utensils to be distributed, it seemed that we were always the last to receive anything, if at all. The situation was such that for months my children had begged me, "Please, Gogo, please, can't we leave this place? Can't we go away?" If I resisted the management's demands, I was afraid this pressure would intensify, with my children being the ones to suffer.

So I sat there and thought, long and hard.

There was no easy resolution, but after long consideration, I saw there was just no other way: my immediate family and I had to leave. The decision was so painful though, that for three full days I couldn't eat. I cried and cried and cried. I prayed and meditated, day and night.

When the day of my departure finally came, my heart broke. As the children from the cottages realized I was leaving Clouds, many of them came running over, crying and screaming, "Don't go, Gogo, don't leave us!" Some actually hung from my legs to prevent me from leaving. It just broke my heart; there is no other way to put it.

So, in February 2011, I left with fourteen of my children while still awaiting paperwork for the other four. We didn't go very far, just down the road, but the conditions of the new place were very different from what we had established at Clouds. The new home was a small, government-built, two-room house in a low-income area called a Location. In South Africa, "Location" refers to an area of housing for the poor, usually on the edges of town. During Apartheid, these areas were reserved for blacks, and while Apartheid has officially ended, the Locations are still very poor and downtrodden, with cramped conditions, overcrowding, and little space for play or gardens (along with having all the other problems that come from poverty and marginalization).

Luckily we do have help from the surrounding community. There is a man, Stephen, whom I immunized as a toddler and who now owns a local shop. Whenever I go there, he asks me, "Gogo, what do you need? How can I help?" And he gives us groceries and staples, whatever he can spare. Then there is the magistrate, a kind soul who is very supportive of us; every fifteenth of the month he brings us groceries—such kindness! So many beautiful souls around us.

Yet even with the help, our new situation is rather challenging. Social Services continues to approach me, asking if I can take in yet more children. But as much as I want to, how can I? At Clouds we had space and support from different groups; people came to give the children workshops, to play with them, or to do educational activities. But in our new home, I don't have any of these resources.

After our move, I went to see my brother in Durban and told him what had happened with Clouds. "Abe," he said, "think about it this way. When a road is built, it's the bulldozer that removes the obstacles and clears the path; without it, there would never be any road. But once that road is built, you don't need the bulldozer anymore. In fact, you don't even want it on your road—or do you?" That made me think. "You speak like our father used to," I replied, and the two of us smiled.

It wasn't particularly flattering to be compared to a bulldozer, but I thought he made a good point. Sometimes it takes one person to start something and another person to run with it. We all have different talents and roles to play, and isn't it ultimately God who is in control anyway? Maybe my brother was right; maybe in the end all that happened was for the best. Also, when I hear what my children say about our family and about me, I know that it was the right decision to leave Clouds. Ntombi, one of my daughters who came to me when she was a baby, said that when I first hugged her she just knew that she was "home." Zonke said that I am "everything" to the children; Nellie talks about how important it is to know that even if we can't always help in our family, we always try; and Thangeka calls the love in our family "amazing" and "unforgettable." Of course, the mother in me is very proud to hear these things. But more importantly, it shows that the children feel secure, at home, and at ease. They know that they are part of a true family, and that is vital to me. The conditions may be hard, but staying together as a family has proven to be the best solution.

And yet, I have twenty-one children living in this two-bedroom house. The lack of space makes even simple tasks complicated. For example, we cannot sit around a table and have a meal together as a family. Some sit in the kitchen, some on the floor, and some have to go outside. There is no proper place for the small children to play, or for the teenagers to find privacy. Even more difficult is that the children need to be able to grow wings and become educated. In a place so small, there is no room to focus and to study, much less to have somebody come in to help with the homework. The simple truth is that we need a bigger home.

And as is true so often in life, when there is adversity and need, there are also people who answer—for no other reason than to help. If there is one miracle I have been fortunate enough to witness many times in my life, it is the miracle of generosity. This time the first step has been taken by my dear friends Thanissara and Kittisaro. It was a true blessing to have met these two people during my time at Clouds. Thanissara and Kittisaro are Buddhist practitioners who built Dharmagiri, a hermitage and retreat center in a rural area close to Underberg. They are truly amazing human beings, and their charismatic and compassionate way has helped many, many people in our community. When I was at Clouds, they provided financial support for us and occasionally came over to discuss how to best help a particular worker or child. They also greatly helped in our efforts to reach out to the local people suffering from AIDS. Over the years, the three of us became close friends, and now they have come to my aid again.

When they saw how cramped we were in our new quarters, they immediately helped expand the place a bit. And in another act of astonishing kindness, Thanissara, Kittisaro, and their friends started a fundraising campaign to help us get a new property. The new nonprofit organization I started to be able to collect funds for the project is called Kulungile. Kulungile means "It is OK; it is good." The name is not wishful thinking; it simply speaks the truth. Every day that I empty myself, the Lord fills me anew, and I can dish out His love. Kulungile—it is well. Every day I can go on without getting bogged down, and I can see my children smile and grow. Kulungile—it is OK. What happens to all of us ultimately lies in His hands, and I know He will help. Kulungile—it is good.

8

Empty Hands

Looking back at my life, I am filled with excitement and gratitude for what I've had a chance to learn and experience. I am just amazed by the grace the Lord has bestowed upon me! Just think about it. I grew up in a culture that suppressed women and didn't value education; and yet, I was given a chance to go to school and become a nurse. I grew up a poor Zulu girl in a poverty-stricken part of the world; and yet, I got to travel around the world and meet His Holiness the Dalai Lama. How utterly amazing! How extraordinary!

All my life, I have been blessed to know people I could learn from, people who taught me skills, who taught me love, who taught me clarity. I've drawn so much strength from their support.

I am also grateful for all the challenges I have encountered, for they have allowed me to grow into the person I am. Challenges keep us on our toes; they awaken our creativity and open our mind. When we can meet and overcome a challenge, it sharpens our skills and strengthens our confidence; and even when we can't find a solution, a challenge will teach us how to let go and trust in Him to solve it. How very lucky I am to have been presented with as many challenges as I have. Every one has been a chance and an opening.

I am thankful too for all I have learned from the different religions. Again, what an amazing grace. I grew up with little spirituality in my life, and then I had the good fortune to find the Christian faith. Later on I also had the chance to experience benefits from other religions, such as Buddhism. Among the many insights gained from my Buddhist friends, there is one that has become especially important for me: do not judge. A judgmental attitude closes our heart and our mind. It builds walls between people and cuts us off from all that nourishes us. It is very sad for me to see people who look down on others, for they are truly blind. So much suffering has been created when, say, people from one religion look down upon people from another religion, or when one race looks down upon another.

As a nurse, I have seen hundreds of babies being born, and I have seen hundreds of people die. And if there is one thing I am absolutely sure of, it is this: we are all in this life together. Whether we acknowledge it or not, we truly are one big family, and we stand together and we die together.

As a child, I was very lucky that I could still experience a culture in which the understanding of ubuntu was still alive. We truly are who we are through our community. When we help another person, we truly help ourselves, and when we do something that makes us grow, it benefits the community. There is no difference. People sometimes call me "selfless" because I have done so much for other people; while that is very kind of them, I don't think they fully understand. What would it make me if I ignored the suffering of others, if I cut myself off? Serving the community is an expression of the exact same desire that made me challenge my station in life; there is no difference. Working for others and for ourselves, the energy flows from the same source. When we can't see this, we are prone to live a life that's based on fear instead of faith that things can be better in the world.

There may be many secrets to happiness, I don't know. Here is mine: every night, I take a little time to let go of the previous day. Every night I empty my hands. And every day, I try to fill them with love and then spend all the love until my hands are empty again.

I always tell my children to not bother Him with things they can do themselves. "God is very busy. He has so much work. You go and try first, and only if you truly can't find a solution do you hand it over to Him. Then you can relax and be excited to see how He will solve the problem." And in the end, He will, He always does. All we have to do is to empty our hands so that we can receive His love.

Afterword

Kittisaro *and* Thanissara

In late March 2013, we launched an Indiegogo campaign to fundraise to find a suitable house for Sister Abegail and her children. For a long time we were aware that Abe and the kids needed a new home, but the means of finding one seemed out of reach. Since our arrival in South Africa in 1994, we had continually fundraised to help launch AIDS response initiatives, educational support, and community development in our local rural area. We had received fantastic help from communities like San Francisco Insight, London Insight, Buddhist Global Relief, and the Libra Foundation. But at that point, we didn't feel we could ask for more. Instead, we tried to do what we could from our own means, while also helping alleviate Sister Abe's situation by having the kids come over to Dharmagiri to play in its spacious grounds.

Over New Year of 2013 we co-taught a retreat at Dharmagiri with our dear friend Andrew Harvey. Around the same time Abe and the kids came over to share a meal and take some time out from their crowded living situation. Andrew was so moved by meeting Sister Abe and hearing of her situation, that he announced that we must find a way to secure a new home for her and the children. While Andrew offered to help advertise a funding campaign, another longtime friend, who was visiting at the same time, recommended Kulungile to a UK charity they had helped found, which covered a substantial part of the overall cost.

With this encouragement, we launched the Indiegogo crowdfunding campaign with the target of $50,000 and began printing T-shirts and cards for the "perks" promised to donors. At the same time, another dear friend, Chihiro Wimbush of Oakland, California, who is an accomplished cinematographer, visited and made a wonderful video of Sister Abegail and her teenagers for the campaign. (This is still available to see on the Indiegogo site under the name Kulungile.)

In the end, through the generosity of 272 Indiegogo donors, alongside many others who gave independently, including Andrew's supporters, and the great generosity of our friend's charity, we were able to raise over $150,000, way over and above our target. This enabled us to make an offer on a beautiful house on the edge of Underberg. With the help of a very kind local realtor, Sue Acutt, the purchase went through without any difficulty.

By September 2013, Sister Abe and the kids had moved into their new home. There was great joy all around as we basked in the warmth of all the generosity, the beauty of the new house, and the glow of Sister Abe's great faith in the goodness of the Lord that Kulungile: "All will be well!"

We were also able to buy much of the furniture in the house, as well as some of the gardening equipment, and secure the ongoing help of the gardener, Mbuso. The house is spacious, light, and welcoming. It has a large building next door that we converted to more bedrooms and a great granny flat for Sister Abe. It has a very large garden, an orchard, and a wonderful vegetable patch and space for chickens. It also has many lovely shrubs, roses, and all manner of colorful flowers at the end of a sweeping driveway that is sealed at night by a large iron gate nestled into a hedge and a secure fence that offers protection and safety. All we need now is to upgrade the dilapidated rondavel, which is the round thatched African dwelling on site, so we can welcome you to visit us all at Kulungile and at Dharmagiri! Until then, *Hamba kahle*—Go well!

To help support Sister Abegail and Kulungile, A Loving Home for Vulnerable Children, please contact us at: kulungile108@gmail.com. To see the new house, please visit YouTube—Kulungile Care Centre—made by Clifton Film Academy, Clifton School, Durban.

Acknowledgments

This little book was made possible by the generosity and support of many wonderful people. I feel deep gratitude for my friends Thanissara and Kittisaro, who inspired me to tell my story and connected me to the people who helped create it; to Jenny Rogers and Wisdom in Action and Wise Giving, who enabled me to come to San Francisco, where I met so many wonderful friends; to Jürgen Möllers and his company, Storyzon, that helped write this book; to North Atlantic Books and their wonderful publishing team for appreciating my story and sharing it with a wider audience, especially Janet Levin, Tim McKee, Jasmine Hromjak, Mary Ann Casler, and Hisae Matsuda; to Pam Weiss and Eugene Cash for their ongoing support; to Eva Ruland and Andreas Jones for their wonderful graphic design; to Rachel Markowitz and Adrienne Armstrong for copyediting and proofreading; and to Stefano Massei for his amazing photos. This book is truly the fruit of the warm spirit that brought together many beautiful and creative people.

Thank you for all you have done!

SACRED ACTIVISM SERIES

SACRED
ACTIVISM SERIES

Heart in Action

When the joy of compassionate service is combined with the pragmatic drive to transform all existing economic, social, and political institutions, a radical divine force is born: Sacred Activism. The Sacred Activism Series, published by North Atlantic Books, presents leading voices that embody the tenets of Sacred Activism—compassion, service, and sacred consciousness—while addressing the crucial issues of our time and inspiring radical action.

*The More Beautiful World
Our Hearts Know Is Possible*
Charles Eisenstein

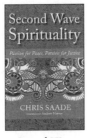

*Second Wave
Spirituality*
Chris Saade

Pioneering the Possible
Scilla Elworthy

Spiritual Democracy
Steven Herrmann

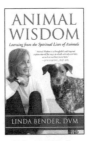

Animal Wisdom
Linda Bender

Time to Stand Up
Thanissara

The Sacred Activism Series was cocreated by Andrew Harvey, visionary, spiritual teacher, and founder of the Institute for Sacred Activism, and Douglas Reil, executive director and publisher of North Atlantic Books. Harvey serves as the series editor and drives outreach efforts worldwide.